FINDING NEW
Meaning IN LIFE

Marcia Griffin & Paul McQuillan

Published by:
Wilkinson Publishing Pty Ltd
ACN 006 042 173
Level 4, 2 Collins St Melbourne, Victoria, Australia 3000
Ph: +61 3 9654 5446
www.wilkinsonpublishing.com.au

International distribution by Pineapple Media Limited
(www.pineapple-media.com)   ISSN 2200-9884

Creator: Griffin, Marcia, author.

Title: Finding new meaning in life / Marcia Griffin &
                  Paul McQuillan.

ISBN: 9781925265743 (paperback)

Series: WP discovery series.

Subjects: Self-actualization (Psychology)
                  Mind and body.
                  Life skills.
                  Logotherapy.

Dewey Number: 158.1

Photos courtesy of iStockphoto.com.

CONTENTS

About the Authors 4

Introduction 7

About Life, Meaning
and Logotherapy 11

Optimism 19

Purpose 25

Responsibilty 35

Decisions 45

Integrity 55

Uniqueness 65

Learning 73

Balance 81

Risk 91

Self-Belief 101

Perspective 111

Vision 121

Energy 129

Resilience 139

Epilogue: Attitude
of Gratitude 147

The Story Behind
This Book 155

Footnotes 158

Index 159

ABOUT THE AUTHORS

Marcia Griffin

has triumphed over a number of challenges including divorce and financial difficulties. Her business skills were recognised when she became the first Telstra Business Woman of the Year in her home state of Victoria, in Australia. She achieved this award by starting a business from zero and growing it into a business with multi-million dollar turnover and nearly 5000 sales consultants throughout Australia and New Zealand. Her first book *High Heeled Success* documented this part of her life journey.

Prior to growing this successful start-up business, Marcia had been a secondary school teacher in English, History and French. Following that, she was a Research Economist with the Australian Wool Corporation. In this role she travelled the world and also acquired further university degrees!

Marcia's qualifications are Bachelor of Arts, Diploma of Education, Bachelor of Commerce and MBA (preliminary).

Her childhood on a sheep and cattle farm gave her a strong work ethic and she believes also prepared her for the challenges of life. In moving from an academic and corporate background to the world of entrepreneurship, Marcia had to rethink her attitude and change much of her thinking.

Marcia has always been passionate about the need to reach out and encourage others to achieve at their highest level, in whatever they choose to do or be. She is now a Director on a number of company boards, she has just sold a business she founded www.griffin+row.com and mentors young people and CEOs.

Through these varied roles, she has learned that the most productive businesses and people are those who can see real meaning in what they do and have closely aligned values. As it is estimated that less than 20% of the workforce is in that space, Marcia believes that the challenge of finding a meaningful life is ongoing and more important than ever before, as a new, highly aware, educated and globally connected generation seek meaning in their lives.

Marcia is a founding Director of the Viktor Frankl Institute as she believes the philosophy of Viktor Frankl is inspiring and enduring.

She is a proud Australian and believes that living in a western democracy is not a privilege that should be taken for granted. She believes that we need to give back, we need to be our best and, most importantly, make life a fulfilling and fun journey!

Marcia enjoys life to the fullest, is vitally interested in politics, loves to ski, appreciates architecture and design and exercises every day!

She lives in Melbourne, Australia.

Paul McQuillan

is a counsellor and psychotherapist who specialises in logotherapy, a path of life and therapy developed by Viktor Frankl. He speaks regularly to executive groups and provides individual counselling and mentoring to busy executives.

He is the current Director of the Viktor Frankl Institute Australia and Director of Lifechange Therapies (www.lifechange.net.au) – the teaching arm of the Institute.

So why logotherapy – meaning centred therapy?

Paul's careers form a rich tapestry. He has been a member of a religious order, a high school Principal in three states of Australia and a school system administrator in both Darwin and Brisbane. His first book was written as a text for the Queensland Computer Mathematics Syllabus in Year 12, well before Microsoft Windows and the internet. The second, Encountering the Mystery, focussed on the profound human capacity of connecting with the mystery of life itself. It was only a short step from there to the depth of Frankl's psychological insights.

That explains the logo, or meaning part of his passion. But why therapy? Paul tells this story to explain:

"Some years ago, while looking after Year 12 students in a large boarding school I ran across Tim, a regular absconder. Tim broke most rules by returning late, not going where he had said he would on a weekend and perhaps should have been stood down. I had a sense that the young man was good at heart and struggling. One evening, after yet another episode I took the time to sit and talk one to one.

His mother was a single parent who lived close by really, so the school environment was more for socialisation than need. During the conversation, which was making little headway, I suggested I role play what his mum might say to him now and ask him to respond. Eventually I asked the question 'why do you do this to me, I love you?' and Tim fired right back 'I love you and I hate you'… I waited…. 'because you lied to me'. This was the key and story tumbled out.

Mum had always told him his father had died in an accident in another state, and Tim had somehow found out he was in fact alive and in prison. It was a healing moment. We worked with the school counsellor, and eventually mother and son were reconciled. What could have been a personal disaster was avoided by first listening, then going deeper and finally changing. I was rapt in the power of positive/searching therapy from that time on. It took longer to progress to being a professional, years in fact, but Tim began the journey for me."

In his search for therapy that could dig deep into what was really happening in his clients lives Paul found that Viktor Frankl's method of therapy had the greatest authenticity for him.

Paul is passionate about logotherapy and its belief in the meaning and uniqueness of every life. He believes every human being can overcome almost any obstacle in life, or take an attitude of strength to the unavoidable.

He is happily married and works as a therapist in Brisbane, Australia.

INTRODUCTION

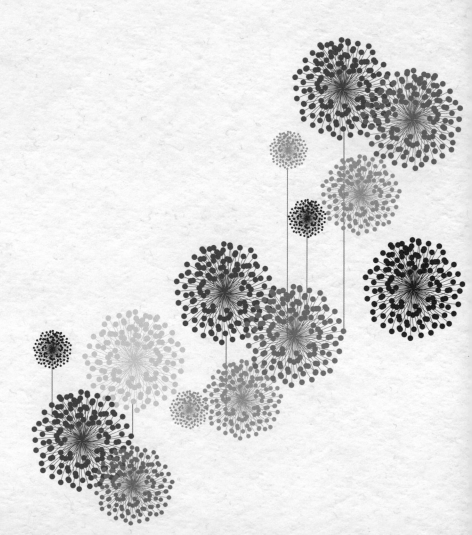

Most of us have had times in our lives when we have had a sense of despair, feelings of hopelessness and self-doubt. The higher we set our goals, the deeper the feelings of despair can be.

I have experienced numerous ups and downs. Consequently, I have been a great reader of motivational books and listened to numerous speakers on the subject of personal motivation. **The quest for living a bigger and more fulfilling life and the desire to inspire others to live and work at their best have always been powerful drivers for me.**

It was, however, a particular set of circumstances that encouraged me to co-write this book. Two people, very close to me (and both highly intelligent and successful) were suffering from depression. Both had admitted themselves to nearby clinics and so I spent time visiting each of them and listening to their concerns and feelings of hopelessness. One of those people had been given a copy of Viktor Frankl's *Man's Search For Meaning*.

I picked up the book on his bedside table – apparently a friend had suggested he purchase and read it. He had taken the first step but not the second!

My friend was on a large dose of anti-depressants and felt no desire to read this or any other book.

Out of curiosity and wondering if this was simply another motivational book, I picked it up and could not put it down.

As I became more and more engrossed, I realised that what **Viktor Frankl was writing about were eternal truths that apply as much in today's world as they applied at the time he wrote his book, over 50 years ago.**

I saw a deep connection between all that I had learned about the power of having meaning, values, an optimistic attitude to life and good mental health.

What I learnt from this powerful book, ironically sitting in a psychiatric clinic, was that while all the motivational books I had read had all served some purpose, simply having a positive attitude is not enough. Viktor Frankl wrote of something much deeper than that and in doing so recognised that in real life we sometimes have reasons not to feel positive, but that we all have the capacity to deal with the challenges of life. **He believed that we all have the choice to find meaning out of even the most difficult times in life.** His message was deep, powerful and authentic, after all, not only was he a psychiatrist by training, but he had lived through and survived the horrors of the Nazi concentration camps.

When I had finished reading the book I had a deep yearning to learn more about logotherapy – Viktor Frankl's methodology in helping people have mentally healthy lives. I felt that while I had come some of the way in my own life to achieving a sense of purpose and set of values, I wanted to search further and deeper. As I listened to my two friends' feelings of despair, I realised that, in addition to my instinctive and learned beliefs about purpose, there was also a strong psychological argument for believing that having a purpose can be a powerful antidote to depression and feelings of hopelessness. Drugs (prescribed or self-medicated) are a short-term solution that many people seem to use as a long-term solution, without solving the real problem. These drugs have started to play such a role in our society that statistics now show that more people are dying from prescribed than unprescribed drugs. It is estimated that one in six people in the Western World is on some form of anti-depressant.

A recent study in Baltimore, the results of which were quoted in the *Journal of Clinical Psychology*, concluded that anti-depressants are commonly used in the absence of clear evidence based indications (of mental disorders).

Western society seems to have sunk into a victim mentality, where qualities such as resilience, perseverance, integrity and responsibility are being overlooked. I believe this societal change is for the worse. We need books, leaders, thinkers and individuals who promote these personal qualities if we are to move forward as a healthy society. We need to be optimistic about the intrinsic capability of human beings to overcome life's challenges.

Whenever we reach out to others to encourage them to achieve their goals, and follow their dreams and passions, we are in fact assisting them in their quest for a purposeful life. **We can all live lives that maximise our capabilities and give us a deep sense of purpose and fulfilment, if we follow some principles which are well within our grasp.**

I was fortunate to find my co-author, Dr Paul McQuillan. Paul is a Doctor of Franklian Psychology, and a logotherapy practitioner. I undertook a brief course with Paul and became totally fascinated by the fact that logotherapy is a powerful tool for keeping us on track on the journey of life. I wondered how my beliefs stacked up and whether the tools I had picked up from my life were enough! So Paul and I began a conversation that grew into a book!

There is a saying: *When the student is ready, the teacher will appear.* In a way, Dr McQuillan was the teacher who came along for me!

In life I have had great fortune and like all of us, some misfortune. Over the years I have sought out many tools and mentors to assist my thinking and when necessary to turn my thinking around. My encounter with *Man's Search for Meaning*, Logotherapy and Paul McQuillan has eclipsed all those previous books and ideas.

Logotherapy provides a way of turning despair on its head. It teaches that, in a meaningful approach to life, the central question we all confront is not 'What do I want from life?' but rather 'What does life ask from me now?' Once we realise it is I and no one else who is asked, we are on the road to strength, courage and recovery.

There is no doubt that in a world of instant and often baseless celebrity, a general attitude of entitlement rather than personal responsibility, as well as destructive and often cruel political or religious leadership, we need positive tools and an abiding set of principles to help us weave through the maze of life. Logotherapy offers this in a non-judgemental, supportive and encouraging manner.

Equally at a time in history when we have never been more globally connected through the internet many of us, young and old, feel disconnected from each other and society, as we have less and less face to face contact. At this time it has become even more important to have a set of abiding values to ensure that we live life to the fullest and remain connected to ourselves!

Life is the most precious gift we have. **The journey is short, but it can be packed with all the great things that having purpose provides—a reason to face each day with excitement, openness and a sense of adventure.**

I hope you enjoy our conversations and that the ideas we discuss, support you on your journey through life.

— Marcia Griffin

ABOUT LIFE, MEANING AND LOGOTHERAPY

I think I saved a life yesterday.

As far as I know this is the first life I have saved. Anyway, at the very least, I saved someone from a life-threatening situation.

We had taken the Limited Express for Himeji on the Hanshin line in Kobe, Japan. In fact we had to run to catch that train but decided to make the effort for no better reason than it was just pulling in to the station, and the next train home might be ten minutes away. So we jumped on to the first available car, right at the front of the train.

When we reached our stop at Nagata he was there. My wife sees him first, an old gentleman, walking stick in his right hand to support himself on that side. However, he is listing so badly to the left that he uses the train itself to provide support with his left hand against the first car. This is all that stops him from falling. Twice he tries to move away from the train and use the stick, only to stagger left and again support himself by placing the left hand against the first car. All the time he is making some forward progress along the car and towards the station exit. The doors close.

The conductor, six cars back, calls loudly over the public address for him to step back behind the white line, and safety.

There is one final but futile attempt to be steady, but the left-leaning tendency remains and he heads again for the train, this time towards the gap between cars one and two. As he is about to fall to the platform and roll between the cars I move forward and grasp his left arm, pushing him to the right. His stagger in that direction at least means a "safe" landing on the platform but away from the train. Thankfully my wife reaches out as well and takes his right arm, stopping the fall. We sit him down as the train rolls on towards Nishidai, its next stop.

I do not know this old man and my Japanese is severely limited, good enough for a cup of coffee but not for conversation. Fortunately my wife is Japanese and **we are able to talk to him and calm him.** In a short time we learn so much about this wonderful man.

He has been celebrating his 85th birthday and admits he has had one drink (in fact probably three or four) too many. He has

no children and lives alone. He is a singing teacher, a good one, who once led a singing group in Carnegie Hall.

It was his old singing group from Carnegie Hall days that had invited him to celebrate the birthday. He was touched by this and very much enjoyed the atmosphere and hospitality. In Japanese culture it is difficult to refuse the offer of a drink in such circumstances for fear of insulting the host. So he had a little more than was wise.

On another trip he remembers being at the Statue of Liberty on 9/11, the day the Twin Towers came down.

He is grateful for the assistance as we slowly begin to negotiate two elevators and various passageways from the station to the surface and his bus stop. It is not a short journey and by the time we have taken it, after a good half hour, he is more in control walking with his stick and able to catch the bus home.

There are a number of lessons about logotherapy in this story and Marcia and I will expand on them as you read this little book. Lesson one is the importance of life itself. **Every life has meaning, which is why our instinct is always to preserve it if we can.** I did not know this old man, I will probably never see him again, so why not leave things to the train conductor and take the risk that his fall between the cars will be noticed and he will be rescued before the train moves off? The answer is the value of life itself.

The second lesson in this story is each person's need to express that unique meaning that each life has. As we age, this often becomes a reflection on our legacy. What we have experienced and achieved can never be taken away, not by death itself. His legacy led our wonderful old man to the city, to accept the hospitality of his former colleagues and to simply reflect on what had been. However, unbeknown to him, his life and his risky departure from the train provided a new meaning for both me and my wife at that time. He could not have realised how his life had given meaning to others in that way. **Helping another human being,** focusing outwards to another, was in this case instinctual, but on reflection personally therapeutic. Our accidental encounter renewed my resolve to help others and perhaps, through this book, his story might provide hope for people he has never met.

Lessons number three and four are a package. Much of life is in reality quite accidental — a series of chance encounters. We could indeed have decided to wait for the next train. Finally, we can never know the full impact of our life on others, whether for better or for worse. This wonderful old gentleman's life provided meaning for ours.

This book is a conversation about life and logotherapy.

Life is often about our capacity to turn tragedy into triumph. To triumph we have to use what logotherapy calls "the defiant power of the human spirit." We have this capacity within each of us, and sometimes, when there is no choice, no way to avoid the pain and suffering in a particular event or circumstance; it is all we have. Life never guarantees happiness, but it does offer each of

Life never guarantees happiness, but it does offer each of us meaning.

us meaning. That is the context of the conversations contained in this book.

Logotherapy was developed in the 1930s by Viktor Frankl. Frankl considered the psychological approaches of both Freud (the founder of psychoanalytic therapy) and Adler (the founder of individual psychology, which is the forerunner to many of today's psychological approaches) as too restrictive.

Freud's insight was that the early years of life certainly shape each of us into the person we become in adult life. Frankl accepted that, but always insisted that it could never completely determine the person. There is always choice. We can decide to be different. Freud further suggested that our will to satisfy our personal desires was the strongest human motivation, the will to pleasure. Frankl challenged this, believing that we can never be fully satisfied by pursuing pleasure. **Human beings must have meaning in life to be satisfied and finding that meaning is our greatest desire.** He believed we can indeed be pushed by drives such as the will to pleasure, or the need to satisfy our basic instincts, to overcome hunger or thirst or just to survive. However, none of those will fully satisfy in the long run, until we recognise our greatest need. We are pulled by meaning.

Adler also believed that there was more to the human being than simply self-satisfaction. He suggested that part of life's journey was to work out our place in society and who we are in conjunction with those around us; the will to power. Frankl again accepts the reality of our pursuit of power and status, but insists we can never be satisfied only by that. Money, fame and success are all chimeras unless they have real meaning and real meaning has to be about more than the self.

Both Freud and Adler's Viennese schools of psychotherapy provide the foundation for much of today's psychology.

Frankl established the third Viennese school, which he called logotherapy. Logotherapy could be described as the *will to meaning*. Frankl's insight was to understand that the study of real human capacity requires more than any one single psychological approach. While accepting the insights of each therapeutic approach, he insisted that each of us has uniquely human qualities which enable every person to go beyond the norm, to take an attitude to any situation, and to choose to respond rather than be driven to do so. In contrast to Freud's method of *Psychoanalysis* (looking to the past to explain who we are), Frankl called his methodology *Existential* Analysis. **That is an analysis of our present existence to determine who we wish to be.**

Logotherapy rests on three major assumptions:

1. Life always has meaning. Life has meaning under all circumstances and at all times. There is something instinctive in the human being that leads us to want to preserve life, both for ourselves and also for those whose lives we see to be in danger. Who would not try to rescue the baby from the burning building, for instance? Logotherapy insists on the meaning of life as a reality.

2. The greatest desire of the human being is to find meaning. Since they have been on this earth, human beings have grappled with fundamental questions such as 'Why am I here?', 'How should I live, given that I must die?' and 'Is there something beyond just my own existence, an overall meaning to life itself?' Logotherapy does not provide answers. It recognises that each person must grapple with and find answers to these questions.

3. Human beings have freedom of choice. The human being always has the capacity to take a choice, to take a stand. We have the capacity to choose meaningful directions in our life and something within us will make us uncomfortable with choosing anything else in the longer term.

Frankl's' **psychiatric credo** held that the human being is always capable of making a choice. Even behind the tragedy of severe brain damage or mental disability, the fundamental human being was still there. If these mental curtains are too dense to penetrate, then logotherapy is not the appropriate treatment, but the essential human being is still there.

The task of the logotherapist is not to present a blueprint for a meaningful life but to realise that each person and each answer is unique. It aims to assist the client in the search for him/herself.

Frankl was once asked what the difference was between psychoanalysis and logotherapy. Before responding, he asked the questioner to describe psychoanalysis. He did so in these terms: *In psychoanalysis, the person lies on a couch and speaks of things that are difficult to talk about*. Frankl responded that, in logotherapy, the client can indeed sit upright in a chair but can then sometimes hear things that are difficult to hear.

There is no cure for life itself, and we do not know from one day to the next what challenges it may bring. Our only choice is to respond to life, to answer the question *"what does life ask of me now?"*

Kate, a single mother with a three-year old daughter, has been a client of mine for quite some time now. We meet and talk whenever she feels the need. Her life has been a patchwork of broken relationships, a tough home life, including being out of home for long periods from the age of 14. When she began therapy she came regularly, as she said "I have tried counselling many times but always gave up, I am going to stick with it this time."

presenting at his clinic was due to frustration with the human search for meaning in life. In fact, the root problem was neither physical nor psychological at all. It was simply a problem that presented with physical or psychological symptoms, brought on by a lack of meaning and direction in life. It is brought on by asking the wrong question about life, by asking *"what do I want from life now?"* and hence by providing a wrong answer, *"life should not be this way"*.

Western society has learned to expect a "cure" for any of life's "dark" feelings. Depression and anxiety are increasing problems as are substance abuse and addictions. I have had numerous clients who define their substance abuse as "self-medicating", only to find that this is simply a cul-de-sac in addressing life's challenges.

Certainly some depression and anxiety can have a physical cause. At other times the cause is drugs and the "self-medication" administered by the individual. In both cases prescribed medications are appropriate. However, if the real cause is in fact a problem with life itself, then a therapy that addresses life's deepest questions is called for. That is, logotherapy.

When the search for meaning is frustrated or avoided over a long period, the person descends into a sort of vacuum of meaning in day to existence. (Frankl called it the *existential* vacuum). This is characterised by boredom, addictions and a general malaise with life itself.

Frankl also often wrote about what happens to a whole society when it asks the wrong

She has. We have had numerous sessions and have completed intensive work. I said to her towards the end of our regular sessions "Kate, you know yourself very well, and you also know all the answers for what life requires just at the moment. You just don't like some of them." She understood that, and has set directions on life that are best for her daughter, but at significant personal cost.

The task of the logotherapist is to ensure that **the person (the client) is assisted with the search for meaning and is uncomfortable unless meaning is being generated through the way they are living life.**

Frankl's work as a psychiatrist led him to believe that at least 20% of psychiatric illness

question about life ("*what do I want from life?*") and as a result comes up with the wrong answer ("*life should not be this way*"). We want to "be happy" but realise we are not. (He called this the '*collective neurosis*[1]').

What happens when society loses its ideals and begins to focus on self-satisfaction; to assume that life should provide a pathway for "happiness", always. Some seek for certainty, to have a pathway that provides a clear answer and direction, eliminating the need to make the tough decisions or to search for meaning. This is the path of fundamentalism in its many forms. Others simply surrender, believing they lack any capacity to influence the world or that their life makes any difference whatever. This is the pathway to depression and even suicide. Still others decide to live only for the present day and to pursue riches and material success, only to find that eventually there is something still missing.

Logotherapy holds that every individual person is unique and important. We all have a unique capacity to respond to life and our response does make a difference. Life itself expects nothing less from us.

One can never know when it is their hour nor what real difference their life makes to others. One of my clients was employed to oversee safety in the workplace across a chain of supermarkets. He was fed up with his role. He longed for something different. My question to him was "so you are sick of saving lives then?" He had never thought of his role as one that could make a difference. Yet as I reflect on saving a life I realise that one life event can retrospectively fill a whole life with meaning.

What does life ask of me now? Frankl was adamant that this question is asked of each individual, that it demands an answer and that only the person who is asked can respond. It is the task of the logotherapist to help clients realise the magnitude of that life task.

Now, I hope you will understand my opening comment: "as far as I know this is the first life I have saved." We can never know what effect, good or bad we have had on others. I hope, as we all do in our hearts, that we have responded positively to life's challenges, knowing always that we have fallen short at times. I hope you enjoy our conversations about life and logotherapy and that they help your own response to life's questions.

— Paul McQuillan PhD, Psy D.
Logotherapist.

OPTIMISM

"For myself, I am an optimist –
it does not seem much
use to be anything else."

— *Winston Churchill*

When I checked the dictionary for a definition of optimism I found something very interesting and in my mind a little challenging:

That the actual world is the best of all possible worlds.

That good must ultimately prevail over evil in the universe.

I am not sure about the first, as it seems to me the world could be a much better place but on the other hand if we accept that first statement, then we may be more at peace with ourselves.

The second part of the definition I find very easy to accept, as I truly believe this.

Sometimes when we think of the past horrors of history and the current tyrannies in the world, it may be easier to believe that evil will prevail. However the weight of history does seem to be on the side of good prevailing.

Optimism, to me, means being realistic about challenges, accepting that the world is not perfect and dealing with that. Optimism is a more powerful concept than positive thinking.

Optimism is about acceptance, belief in opportunity and good outcomes.

It is more proactive, than simply thinking positively and is more realistic.

I, for one, simply can't feel positive 100% of the time but I can feel optimistic that I will get through the challenges and find a way to solve problems. **If the challenge does prove to be impossible then as an optimist I will focus on doing something else.**

I accept that generally in life I have been blessed and so the things I have had to confront – not having children, losing all the money I had ever made at one stage in my life, have been surmountable challenges, largely because I have believed that I would find solutions.

My way of handling not having children has been to seek the company of young people. My very close friend Lizzie helped me with this and over the years I spent many wonderful evenings with her four children. When she died suddenly I committed to keeping that close contact with her children and now grandchildren and often feel the sad irony of the fact that she, not me, should be the person watching and enjoying her family grow and her grandchildren become what she would have been very proud of.

The money challenge was a different one where I simply had to work extremely hard, invest wisely when I did have some savings and spend very carefully. I had some luck also in overcoming this challenge. The luck however was entirely due to taking on challenges in business that seemed almost impossible at the time – i.e. growing a sales team of nearly 5000 women from a zero start! Just as I am an optimist I had a very optimistic mentor who supported my dreams.

Optimism is about acceptance, belief in opportunity and good outcomes.

Optimists are attracted to each other and become more successful for doing so. If we adopt the optimistic approach, and it is a choice, we can move forward and overcome negative, depressing thoughts and situations.

When I read *Mans Search for Meaning* it was this quality of optimism that Viktor Frankl called on in the worst of times in the concentration camp that inspired me.

It was this distinction between having a blindly positive attitude and being realistically optimistic that really attracted me to this incredible book.

Tips for being optimistic:

✓ Accept that most people are trying to do their best

✓ Focus on the beauty of the planet

✓ Look for solutions rather than problems

✓ Seek out people who are optimists

Life always has meaning

Optimism is a good beginning for this conversation. Logotherapy can at first seem a very dark way of looking at life. It affirms that all of us have dark times and tragedy in our lives. That is unavoidable. But even in our best times life needs to have tension and challenge. Unless it has this it becomes an aimless drift into depression and lack of meaning. I will expand on this further when we talk about learning.

It is in our darkest hours that we learn not only to cope but to triumph. So in reality logotherapy provides a significantly optimistic yet a very realistic way to live one's life.

Logotherapists believe that life always has meaning, even under the most difficult and challenging of circumstances. Even in the most abject circumstances life will always have meaning. Surely that is a sign of optimism and hope, always.

Frankl, talking about his own concentration camp experiences, was clear that those prisoners who had the highest chance of survival had a meaning – something to live for in the future. Note that in this circumstance it meant a better chance for survival. The decision to survive or not was often not their own.

What about those who had this dream for a better future but were then eliminated in the gas chambers? Even if the prisoner did not survive they were challenged to meet their final end with dignity. To remain a real human being until the last – that is the ultimate in optimism.

I have seen numerous clients who relate a childhood of suffering and often abuse. Alcoholic-fuelled abuse by parents and step-parents, disowned and unwanted by one parent or another; all of these things can affect a person's life in the future. The genius of logotherapy is to realise that nothing has to be blamed for our life tomorrow. We decide what life means for us from today. All the past does is to have all of us begin at different points.

What is the difference between those who can pick themselves up and move on and not simply survive but indeed decide to thrive in the future? **Frankl says that the real issue is choice.** It must be "this is who I want to be" or "I have decided to be my best and rise above these circumstances". In effect it is a matter of attitude to survive.

I am reminded of one of my clients who had come from Iran via Turkey. His father had been murdered by the regime because

of his political beliefs. He himself had been drafted into the army but realised that his time there would probably be short as people from his ethnic background did not always survive long, particularly once there were live-firing exercises. So one day he asked to leave the camp to collect a pair of glasses, and never returned. He deserted.

After many adventures, tenuous border crossings and occasional lucky escapes he made it to Turkey. Finally he was granted a visa to come to Australia.

When I met this wonderful person he was driving a taxi. He said to me 'sometimes there is little business. When there isn't much happening the drivers stand around and get bored. I try to cheer them up. I tell them surely life is still much better than we had at home'.

So from being in a reasonably privileged position in his country of origin to living on the edge in in his newly adopted country he remained optimistic.

The opening chapter on Optimism tells how you found alternatives in life, how you persevered and in doing so, succeeded. I have to say that some of my clients do not always succeed. However, it does not take away the value of their life nor of what they try to achieve nor the real dignity and nobility in continuing to persevere. As Frankl says "even the unfinished symphonies are beautiful, as are the pathetiques".

So to live with optimism is the most important thing we can do as human beings. We are challenged to live life to the very end and to realise that our life always has meaning even under the most difficult circumstances. A realistically optimistic attitude is one that understands that life always demands a response, even at its most destitute and even at its very end. The response is ours and we must make it.

Now the good news about this for a therapist is that **optimism is one skill that can be grown and trained.** Have you ever said "It always happens to me?" or "I never..." Well, just stopping the negative thoughts and changing the language does great things. It actually changes the brain the scientists say when you can change to "It sometimes happens to me" and "I usually or I often find ..."

So to be optimistic, change the language. When people refer to changing your mindset on something that is really close to the truth. Changing your language will change your mindset.

Healthy Attitude:
Bad things happen to good people.
I can cope with this.

Unhealthy Attitude:
I don't deserve this. Why is this happening to me?

Healthy Attitude:
I have recovered from adversity before, so I can do so this time.

Unhealthy Attitude:
This is too hard – I give up!

Healthy Attitude:
Most of our "good luck" in life is what we have been spared from having to endure.

Unhealthy Attitude:
Why me? It's always me that has to have such bad luck.

PURPOSE

If you don't know where you're going,
you will probably end up somewhere else.

A Meaning Filled Life

Marcia,

Thank you for your reflections on Purpose.

This book is a conversation and I look forward to that. Our conversation will be about how your own philosophy of life and business sometimes runs parallel, and at other times counter to, the powerful insights of Viktor Frankl, into the human being and life itself, which he called logotherapy. Purpose is certainly a core concept, but let's go a little deeper.

Logotherapy is founded on the principle that life always has meaning—at all times, even the most difficult. So even if we have no easily identifiable task to do or even if through disability or other affliction we are unable to achieve even the most basic of tasks, life still has meaning – and Frankl believed that we can find it. So you can see that while purpose provides the best beginning to our conversation, it is incomplete because "purpose" is only one facet of finding meaning.

I am going to respond to your concepts in each chapter from the perspective of a meaning-centred therapist.

So to begin. You are indeed so close to outlining **what a meaningful approach to life demands** and what meaning-centred therapy

— logotherapy — challenges us to confront. On the other hand, I sense there is still a small step to take beyond what you have outlined. Why is that?

I am reminded of that wonderful part in the movie *The Razor's Edge*, where Larry, searching for his own meaning in life, encounters his Indian mentor. He has just arrived in India to be confronted with the stark reality of real poverty. At first he is generous to a little boy begging for money, then another, then more and finally he is pursued by so many seeking a gift that he runs away with the whole entourage now in pursuit. He takes refuge on a barge and meets this simple man with a depth of understanding about life. Naturally enough, their conversation centres on Larry's reasons for coming to India to further his search for meaning. Why India?

"Oh, what was your intention?" his mentor asks.

Larry: "I worked in a coal mine to get the money to come here".

Mentor: "No, that was your purpose. You see if work has no intention, it's not work at all."

What Larry's mentor is telling him is that there is a further dimension to work, beyond

just doing it and beyond having a personal goal to achieve as a result. He states that is the 'intention' that is all important. **In logotherapy, we call it meaning.** The purpose of my work may indeed be to earn a living, but how I do that and what I do, simple or complex as it may be, can have a meaning that is deeper than the deed itself.

Coming back to what you have said about purpose. I agree with you that a goal provides the 'what' and that purpose answers the 'why'. But I would like to take you one step further, because 'meaning' provides the 'who'.

So you see the "whats" and "whys" of life can be similar, indeed even identical to the outside observer. The 'who' is unique. **Each person on this earth is perfectly and absolutely unique.** In recent times the unravelling of the DNA puzzle has emphasised this point. To fully realise our uniqueness in turn imposes an awesome understanding of our task in life.

Who I am is of course determined somewhat by what I do, and for most of us that is intimately tied up with our work. However it is even more than that.

My meaning, if it is to be true to who I really could be, will not only be bigger than me but it will focus outwards on others.

I can only be me by encountering YOU. If I do that well, the intention of my work, and its meaning, spreads beyond myself and my tasks.

Look at it like this. If someone made a movie of my life, and I believe every life is worth that effort, would I be a hero, a villain or simply avoid all responsibility, allowing myself to be flotsam on the sea of life? You give an excellent example of leaders who are self-centred and indeed evil. They have somehow managed to anaesthetise themselves against their conscience. They are now centred only on self and not on others, a pathway to ultimate despair, and this is the opposite of meaning.

So you can see that while purpose provides the best beginning to our conversation, it is incomplete because "purpose" is only one facet of finding meaning.

I am reminded of one of my clients who had a history of failed relationships, alcohol and drug taking. On the other hand, he had been reasonably successful financially. One evening, through a knock at the door from the police, he was asked whether he would take custody of his two-year-old daughter, as the mother was not able to care for her. The police believed him to be the father. In fact, this little girl was the result of a one month encounter between two people living in an oblivion of alcohol drugs and sex. His little girl was the result of a brief "love" tryst with a person he had not seen since. A daughter who up to that point he had not even realised existed.

What to do? What he did do was resign from his full-time job and devote himself completely to bringing up the little girl. In our many sessions together, it became apparent that his purpose in past times had been cen-tred on hiding from life. When not cocooned by alcohol or drugs, it had centred on money and self-interest.

His life until then seemed to lack meaning. **Now, by reaching out to grasp just how great he could be as a human being, life had meaning.** It also had a more difficult financial situation without the compensation of alcohol and drugs.

So you see that purpose can be, as you point out, varied in its impact. It can cause terrible suffering or be centred only on personal gain.

However, real meaning cannot be centred on the self. If it is, our conscience will constantly nag at us to tell us that we have not fulfilled our meaning. It is lack of meaning that underlies much of the depression, despair and addiction we see around us, not lack of purpose as such.

So you are correct when you say that those

without purpose can become victims of depression, despair and addictions. But ultimately it is the lack of meaning that underlies this.

You see, we can have purpose but have no meaning.

A second client came because he had indeed once 'had it all': the business, the marriage and the family. However, it was all taken away through a major business failure and a failure in his marriage. The disintegration of the marriage had been exacerbated by an abject failure in parenting, bordering on abuse as he admitted later, combined with an obsessive concentration on his purpose, the business.

He was in despair. How could he rebuild his life? Try as I might, I could not deflect him from his conviction that his first step in finding a new pathway had to be to rebuild the business and make his fortune, because only then could he build a successful relationship. Yes, he knew in his heart he was too old and physically not strong enough to do what he had done in his youth. He knew in his heart that rebuilding the business was no longer possible, but he remained wedded to that as his definition of who he was. He left therapy still despairing about life.

You see Marcia, this second client had a purpose in life but was now being challenged to find a meaning.

As you point out, it is the hope of most parents that they can have children who become satisfied and happy in their lives. As a therapist, I suggest that at a deeper level we should desire for our children and ourselves to be able to find meaning. It will be their own, their very personal meaning that they find, because no therapist can give it them. They must also continue to search, as meanings can change throughout life.

The search will involve the whole range of human emotions, including happiness, despair and sadness at times. That is positive. Because, as you point out, happiness itself can be fleeting and cannot be pursued as an end in itself, in the same way that anger cannot be pursued as an end in itself.

Your attitude to this unique life, over which you have custody, is the key.

Healthy Attitude:
I am unique. The world will be a better or worse place, depending on how I respond to life.

Unhealthy Attitude:
I am a mere pawn and can make no difference in this world.

Healthy Attitude:
Even the unfinished symphonies are beautiful, as are the pathetiques. (Viktor Frankl)

Unhealthy Attitude:
Success gives me meaning, failure is meaningless.

Healthy Attitude:
I can only find my meaning by encountering others and sharing all of life's emotions.

Unhealthy Attitude:
Happiness is the key, my personal happiness must be pursued.

I look forward to our conversations in this book and trust that we can provide tips for operating in the world, as well as suggestions about healthy and unhealthy attitudes we can take to life itself.

RESPONSIBILITY

Live as though you were living already
for the second time and as if you had acted the first
time as wrongly as you are about to act now.

— *Viktor Frankl*[2]

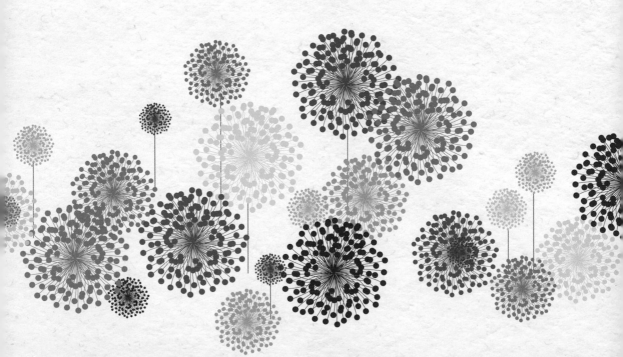

Responsibility is such a great word—made up of the **ability to respond.**

One of life's toughest challenges is learning to take full and complete responsibility for one's decisions and choices. Most of us, as human beings, have this capability but often it is easier to blame others, the government, one's parents, partner, employer or someone else.

Understanding the importance of responsibility is very empowering, as it gives us the opportunity to take our lives into our own hands and change direction if we need to, or simply continue on our happy path, aware that if it is to be it is up to me!

At one stage of my life, I was consumed with self-pity and particularly blamed my ex-husband for my woes—financial and emotional. However, a deeper and more intense analysis of the situation put a very different slant on the challenges I was going through. Essentially, I had handed over to my ex-husband the role of managing our money and most of the rest of our married life.

Of course, when the money had gone he was an easy target for blame. However, I now see that in handing over many decisions to him I had failed to take responsibility for my life and therefore suffered the consequences.

Over the last few years, I have come across a number of people going through the same process of blame, and I can see how this reduces their control over life. Their story is always the same —someone else did it to them:

They were not promoted because their boss did not like them; their marriage ended because their partner did the wrong thing by them; they lost their money because the stockbroker gave them the wrong advice; their parents caused them to be like this...

The endless list of blame goes on. But one thing is missing in all this, and that is the role the individual has played.

Eventually, I started to realise that many of my life challenges were caused by the decisions and choices I had made (who I had married, who I had listened to, whose opinions were important to me). At this point I realised that all these issues had one person at the centre—me!

Of course, no-one wants to admit mistakes and failures, so the easiest target is someone else. And that is generally the people we are closest to—family, spouse, friends and advisors. **The reality is that, for as long as we deflect blame from ourselves, we cannot move forward** and we always have an excuse—our parents, employer, the government.

Recently, I had a car accident that completely destroyed my car. My initial reaction was to blame the trees at the corner of the street for blocking my view and the speed of the oncoming car. The reality was that I took a risk in not waiting for the oncoming car to pass the intersection.

Yes, it was an accident and I did think I had enough time to cross the road. But as I have lived on the same street for ten years and waited at that corner hundreds of times, it was simply an error of judgement. My error. Yes, there would be better vision if the tree was not on the corner; but that is a given and I should have allowed for it, having done that so many times before.

Every day in the media we hear of people making victims of themselves and refusing to take responsibility. I think the most outrageous recent example of this was the captain of the Italian ship who seemed to be in total denial over the cause of the accident but was with his lover at the time of the ship's collision, and then *happened* to fall into a lifeboat before most of the passengers and his crew! There also seemed to have been an order from him to go closer to shore so his family could see his ship and this order contributed to the accident.

In Australia, we recently had the case of the union leader cum politician who, when it was discovered he had spent thousands of dollars of workers' money, had supposedly been a victim himself. He claimed his credit card was stolen; it could not have been him; he did not know these brothels; he'd never been there. He lied to parliament in front of the whole country but, of course, the truth eventually does come out, despite the tears and lies.

The victim mentality which is essentially about failure to take responsibility, is crippling for both individuals and society. **Someone else is always being asked to pay, the individual does not learn, and society continues to be burdened by people who could be contributing to the greater good but never will, because they will not take responsibility.** Many psychologists and parts of the legal system seem to have encouraged this lack of responsibility by allowing the defence of *syndromes*. The last one of these I am aware of, was entitled *the forgotten baby syndrome*. This enabled a young woman to walk away from the death of her tiny baby in a

The victim mentality which is essentially about failure to take responsibility, is crippling for both individuals and society.

hot car in summer! While she may have actually forgotten about her child, this syndrome will no doubt now become a defence for future cases of child negligence.

If we refuse to take responsibility, we also refuse to take the opportunity to change our lives for the better. If it is always someone else's fault, we may not be able to change them but we can change ourselves. The victim approach to life takes away control from our lives and leaves us feeling helpless and even useless.

Sure, there are plenty of things that we can't change or control. There are, however, some great examples of one person being a force for major shifts and major movements that have changed the world. In recent history, Martin Luther King's *I Had a Dream* speech stirred a nation and eventually changed the lives of millions of Americans. The amazing young Pakistani girl Malala stood up for the education of women, only to be shot by the Taliban, and yet she survived and continues on her mission despite the dangers. There are numerous instances of one person changing the world and, while this may not be within our reach, at least it is an indication that anything is possible if we take responsibility.

Sometimes we get opportunities to respond to very strange circumstances. **I have no doubt that the way we respond affects the outcome of the situation and is influenced by something we have learnt.**

After a trip to the beautiful town of Aspen some years ago, I decided to visit New York—a city well up there on my list of favourites. I got there very late. There was a taxi strike and so I found myself on a bus with skis, bags and far too much stuff to handle—particularly as we arrived at the bus station at 2am. Fortunately,

a kind gentleman warned me of the danger of being in that place with so much luggage and also helped me carry it.

I arrived at the locked Hotel Elysée, famous for its Monkey Bar, at 3am and had to wake the concierge by yelling very loudly. I finally got into my triple-bolted room and collapsed into a deep sleep.

Next morning, I was anxious to make the most of my short New York stay, so dragged myself out of bed and started walking down Madison Avenue. It was 10am, the street was busy, and I was still in a bit of an Aspen frame of mind. This meant that my shoulder bag was over my coat—not in its usual city place, under my coat!

As I wandered along, I noticed that two tall black men were walking beside me, so close they seemed to be squeezing my shoulders. I looked from one to the other; they were looking ahead and so I just kept walking, thinking there were plenty of people on the street and perhaps I was imagining the squeeze!

Suddenly my bag felt very light. I looked down, the flap was open and, horror of horrors, my wallet with passport, credit cards, and cash had gone! My new companions were still walking with me. I wanted to yell but thought better of it and, given that Australians were very much in favour in New York then, due to the movie *Crocodile Dundee* and that very large knife, I turned to one of the men and said quietly, but as firmly as my shaking body would allow: "I need that wallet; I am an Australian in New York on my own; it has my passport and all that I need as a traveller".

To my astonishment, the man turned to me and handed me back my wallet. The two men then took off and left me shaking on the pavement in the middle of busy Madison Avenue.

A woman came up to me and told me she had seen the whole thing: the bag being opened, the wallet being taken and then handed back. She was shocked, I was amazed and needed to sit down. I buzzed one of the designer stores — to this day have no idea which one — and was let in by the concierge. I told him and the amazed staff about what had happened; **they had never heard about wallets being handed back!**

To this day I have ruminated on this story. Had I responded differently, I am not so sure that the story would have ended so well. Fortunately, some years before this incident, I had done a short course in managing conflict using the principles of Japanese martial arts. One of the many things I learnt was to respond to aggression quietly. Had I yelled at the potential thieves, I think they would simply have taken off with the wallet and disappeared into the crowd. Instead I treated them as human beings and sought their understanding. They responded. They took responsibility in that moment for my welfare.

We do always have the ability to respond in a variety of ways. **The way we respond is key to how we handle the complexities of life!**

Tips for Responsibility:

- ✓ We cannot control all that happens to us.
- ✓ We all have the ability to respond to circumstances, either positively or negatively.
- ✓ Taking responsibility is the best way to learn, grow and change.
- ✓ Blaming others does not solve our problems.

Be the Person You Can Be

Marcia,

In one famous lecture, Frankl once said that **"if you take man as he is, you make him worse, if you take man as he should be then you can help him be what he can be."** In other words, we need assume human beings can rise above our expectations, much like your two thieves did when they returned your wallet. Let me explain this in the context of our conversation on responsibility.

Your remarks on responsibility provide an excellent second step to our conversation on life and logotherapy. I have said earlier that the foundation of Logotherapy is the belief that life always has meaning; at all times and under all circumstances. Responsibility brings to mind the second concept: that our greatest human desire is to find meaning in our lives.

No therapist can do this for you. **You are the only person who can find that meaning in life and you will do it through taking responsibility for your life.** So the concepts in this chapter are fundamental to that search for meaning.

Responsibility is parallel to this search for meaning and yet a little different. In taking responsibility we have meaning thrust upon us

so to speak. Responsibility is about responding to whatever challenge we may face at a given time. How does life challenge me to respond at this time? How good could I be? How heroic perhaps? It may be more demanding in some ways than the heroism of the battle field, for the heroism of responding to the unchangeable, the incurable disease, the bed-ridden partner, demands a longer-term devotion to duty.

There are particular times where we are called to transcend the self. **To rise above what we might be or even who we have been — to aim for what we know we could be.** To aim for something better than we are and so, hopefully, utilise at least some of the capacity we all have as human beings to respond to whatever challenge life presents.

Once I was watching my aircraft's approach to Kansai Airport on the TV screen. In those days Japan Airlines had a forward camera, so you could see some of what the pilot sees as the aircraft lands. There was a strong crosswind so that, as we approached this small island in the middle of the sea, the plane actually steered at an angle of about 45 degrees to the runway, not directly at it. Only by doing this could the

plane actually get to where it was trying to go — the edge of the landing strip.

It was a scary experience, but we made it. Had we taken what might have seemed the "obvious" or "easy" path we would indeed have missed the safe landing.

You see, what Frankl was saying is that the only way to be fully human is to aim a little beyond what we think is possible. We are challenged to rise above our natural tendency to retreat from difficult but unavoidable circumstances and to take a defiant attitude to them.

Marcia, we all hope that we will have good fortune in life. Good fortune is really the absence of some of the personal challenges others may have been called to face. This is the problem with the positive psychology movement: life is not always 'positive'.

It is very important, of course, to have a model of optimism. This is evidenced by confidence in one's own self-efficacy and the expectation of positive outcomes. Positive psychology and logotherapy both endorse this. What can be missing, however, is a model of optimism for when we are helpless and all seems hopeless. Logotherapy supplies this and calls it 'attitude'.

Logotherapy is not only based on self-confidence and positive expectations but also on the basic truth that the only choice we ever have is to respond to what life brings, right now, today. That is, life challenges us to take full responsibility for the unavoidable.

What are these unavoidable situations?

In essence, they are what we call the 'tragic triad' of death, guilt and suffering. All of these are unavoidable. We will all experience them, that much is certain. All of them call for a response that transcends the self — that is to take an attitude to life that responds to the challenge.

Let's start with suffering. We are all condemned to suffer in life, but we will avoid it when we can, and so we should. As I mentioned, good fortune can be re-interpreted as simply not having had as many personal challenges as others. **None of us want to suffer; but when we are called on to look into the face of adversity and rise above it, that is the real challenge.**

Elsewhere[3] I have told the story of a client of mine, Storm. Storm was the victim of 30 years of domestic violence and eventually left her marriage to escape with her own life intact. Making this decision at an age when most of us would hope for a comfortable retirement left Storm destitute. She also suffered severe ataxia,[4] due to the consistent violence she had experienced.

Taking responsibility for a new life, beginning with nothing, yet being able to approach life with a positive attitude provided me (as her therapist) with an awe-inspiring example of what the human person is capable of becoming. Storm believed life always has meaning, even with the severe limitations that challenged her. She resolved to search for meaning and to take responsibility for what she had left in life. Ultimately that was her 'cure'. Now she continues to campaign on behalf of those who experience similar violence which is often hidden and often manipulative.

There is no 'cure' for life itself, save the capacity we have to search for meaning and to believe we can find it.

The second part of the tragic triad is guilt. All of us, when we suppress our conscience and refuse to take full responsibility, experience guilt in our hearts. We know we could have done better. Meanings are unique to each situation and the decisions we take. Hence our chosen path will always have a meaning. But if the meaning is only for myself, it will leave a vacuum. **Deep down we want our chosen path to be me at my best, displaying my full human potential for good.** Hence we will find it hard to live with what we have done if we do it only for ourselves.

How to overcome this guilt? We cannot relive the past. As you mention, we can choose to blame others for what has happened and fail to admit mistakes and failures. On the other hand, we can take an attitude to guilt. We can learn from our mistakes and resolve to make meaningful decisions in the future. That is, when given the chance next time, we intend to rise beyond what we have been and strive for what we know we can be. To face the aircraft into the wind, so we do land in the right place! That is the meaning of Frankl's advice to "live as though you were living for the second time".

We cannot change what we have done. What we can change is what we do tomorrow.

So don't make a decision now that you know has no meaning. Aim to be a better person and avoid the guilt you will create in the future.

Finally, in the tragic triad, there is death. Death is obviously unavoidable, despite the wonders of medical science. **Logotherapy treats death as important because it means that life is finite.** Hence the attitude we take (responding to what life brings, taking responsibility for each day) is what makes life meaningful.

One of the questions I sometimes ask a client is: What would you do if the doctor told you that you had only one month to live? There are various answers. One client who had come for advice about his relationship responded that he would "go to Morocco" – because he had never been there. He realised quickly that his partner was not included in his real priorities and so that was the issue that was destroying his relationship. However, most people when asked will respond that they want to make peace with family members or those who have been wronged, as well as gathering loved ones around to tell them "I love you. Thank you."

A good follow-up question is: *If they are your priorities, given you have only a month to live, why would you leave these things until you are given your death sentence?* Each day is precious. Why are you not contacting your estranged relative and mending the fences now – before it is too late to do so?

Healthy Attitude:
If I take responsibility for and respond to life's challenges, there is meaning to be found in them. Sometimes bad things happen to good people.

Unhealthy Attitude:
These things should not be happening to me!

Healthy Attitude:
My past mistakes guide me towards better decisions in the future.

Unhealthy Attitude:
I feel guilty for some of my past and so I try never to think about those events.

Healthy Attitude:
The fact that I must die makes each day an important part of my journey.

Unhealthy Attitude:
Just enjoy yourself, you only live once.

A very good motto to live by is: Live as though you were living life for the second time.

DECISIONS

Life is a series of
choices and decisions.

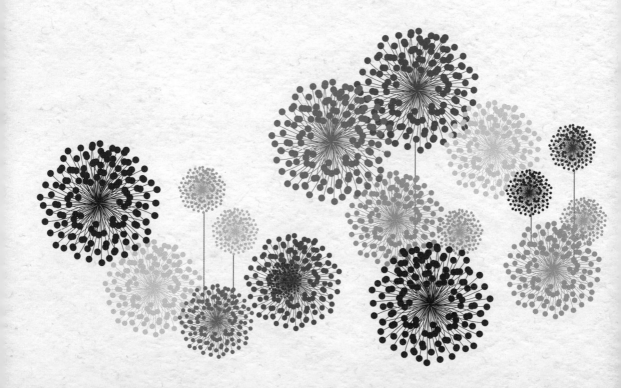

While business may be a daily-problem solving exercise, life is a daily decision-making exercise.

Decisions are not easy, because we often don't know the outcome or the likelihood of the outcome.

Some people defer decisions for a very long time. Their life story reads: *I always planned to leave, change etc., but just did not get around to it.*

Some people live their whole lives in a less than desired place emotionally, physically, financially and spiritually because deciding was too hard. They live their lives as if they were going to have a second go at life.

Paul you suggested in the last chapter to live *as though* you were doing it the second time around. It may be consoling for those who believe in reincarnation that they will do better the second time, but those of us who don't have that belief, had better make the most of the here and now! We don't ever get days, months or years back. So before jumping into something, first think about it. Would you really have been proud of what you are about to do IF you had a second life?

As a mentor, I have listened to CEOs and business owners sometimes procrastinating about business decisions. These decisions are often about an employee. The conversation goes like this: *this person is really not adding value to the business or, worse still, is causing serious problems in the business; but she/he has a lot of knowledge and a replacement will need a lot of training, or is really popular with the other staff, or is a nice person* or similar. Often these are excuses to delay the inevitable. **The longer we take to make decisions, the harder it becomes.**

Once a decision has been made, the conversation is about being relieved: *I wish I had done it earlier and it was not so hard after all.* Generally, the person whose job is under consideration is relieved also, as they will now have a better chance of success in a place where they can add value. Decision-making requires a lot of honesty and clarity and sometimes it's really hard to action the decision.

We often hear people say that they have not regretted what they have done, but have regretted what they have not done!

As I look back on my life, that is exactly how I feel — the only regrets are the things I have not done. But I am making those things I do not do fewer and fewer as life goes on. This is not just because I am getting older, (that is certainly the case), but rather because I approach decisions now with that knowledge in mind.

In my property renovations, exactly the same principles apply. Renovating a house is like the decisions we need to renovate our lives. My reflections and examination of my life are similar to what I have been doing over the last couple of years in a major house renovation. It is a lovely '60s house that has been

neglected but has great bones. What I have been doing is working to keep the good bones of the house while adding some wonderful updated features!

Actually, it's a similar process to a personal renovation — what is working, what does not work and what will work best in the future? The sort of decisions we have to make in life every day.

When I fail to do something that I know would add to a property, but skip because of perceived cost or difficulty, I regret that. So, as I renovate a house now, I do everything that I think will make the property more attractive and more valuable, as I know that the cost of leaving out that change will be higher than including it in the end.

This does not mean there are no compromises in life. As with renovating or building, there is always a more expensive option! In a property renovation, we cannot avoid making decisions. In life, we sometimes do avoid making decisions, because they are too hard or too confronting. But we may be disappointed with the results of such indecision!

The thing that helps me with property decisions is thinking through to the end result.

Just so in life; the questions are: "What if I don't do this?" "What are the consequences?" The great thing is that when we make a decision to do something, and then discover that it's not going to be as wonderful as we thought, we can generally stop or change direction,

You can always choose your response

Marcia,

As always, you make some wonderful points. I certainly agree life is a decision-making exercise. However, you seem to me to contradict yourself. You say that 'we don't ever get days, months or years back' and I agree. Yet you also believe 'most of life's decisions are changeable'. I agree with your first statement but not the second.

A decision is forever, once taken it cannot be changed. What we can do is to take another decision to ameliorate at least some of the damage! I will talk about that later. For now I will concentrate on decisions as such.

Decisions bring us to the third core belief of logotherapy. This last core belief is liberating yet daunting. We always have the capacity to choose our response to life and hence to choose meaningful directions.

Viktor Frankl's psychotherapeutic credo holds that:

> Human beings are always capable of choosing their response to any circumstance in life.

But, you object, what about those who are incapable, those afflicted by mental disorders for instance? The second part of Frankl's credo says that:

> Even behind the tragedy of brain damage or severe mental illness, the human being is still there.

You see, the 'curtain' of illness or damage can be too dense to penetrate, but the 'core' of the human being is always intact; it just may not be possible to see it or to see it only in brief glimpses of reality.

So in this first part of our conversation, we have covered the three key concepts of logotherapy:

* Life always has meaning.

* Our greatest desire is to find meaning in life.

* We have the freedom to choose meaningful responses to life.

So let's talk about decisions.

Most decisions are automatic. We take no notice of them. Breathing, for instance, is automatic. We can notice it if we wish, but normally we do not bother. If we decide to stop breathing, and children sometimes experiment with that, we soon find out that the body rebels.

How often have we taken the wrong turn while driving and ended up in a street we knew simply because it is the way we have always been used to going, but we had not intended to go there this time? We aren't thinking about it, the brain was on auto-pilot. Life itself can also be lived on auto pilot if we are not careful! Another way to look at our driving is that we "decided" to take the wrong turn simply because we did not actually decide anything.

It is really important to realise that even procrastinating is taking a decision. A decision to do nothing! Usually this is not a positive direction.

A meaning-filled life will take meaningful decisions. To make a meaningful decision we first of all need to take account of our values.

Values are our deeply-held beliefs about life itself and particularly about our own life. Most values are inherited, from society, from family, but as we mature some values are entirely our own.

We value stability and a regular income, yet we might stand up for the rights of a colleague in the workplace, even at the risk of our own wellbeing. We would not feel 'right' if we simply kept a low profile and watched a clear injustice perpetrated. Why is this?

Every decision faces three basic questions:

* What is best for me?

* What is best for others?

* What 'ought to be'?

Every decision has a meaning. Values can be in conflict, but the meaning of each decision is a 'one-off'. Who benefits from this decision? If it is only best for me it is likely that it does not pass the test of the other two questions. There is one more question to answer as well, so let's examine that.

I once had a client, a lawyer, who came for advice about his relationship. He had been having an affair that was discovered by his wife. As a result he promised to break it off and not to see this lady again. The lady had supported him as his personal assistant while his business went to the wall and he founded another practice. A stressful time, and he felt he grew apart from his wife as he faced this challenge.

However he had lied when he promised to break it off. The affair continued. They met regularly for coffee, he worked late and they met for a meal and so on. Now he was seeking advice – should he leave his wife, who he felt he no longer loved, for a person who he felt really did understand him? What about the children? He loved them – three kids under 10 years of age. How would they cope? Could he continue to love them? Would life be different? He dissolved into tears each time he thought of leaving the kids.

Our conscience tells us what 'ought to be'. How will we know what "ought to be"? If the meaning is centred only on the self, and fails to consider the broader perspective, then there will be that nagging doubt within us that we could have done it better.

We worked together over a number of sessions, never coming up with an answer. I pointed out that whatever happened, there would be others hurt in this. Something in my client would not allow him to let go of a marriage as he felt it "ought to be" a permanent commitment. We worked on listing who would benefit from each pathway and who would be adversely affected.

Conscience tells us, sometimes by nagging us in hindsight, that a particular decision will have a very selfish meaning. Each decision can lead to a meaning-filled life, but only if its meaning is in accord with our conscience.

In simple terms, a meaning-centred approach to life helps us become a better human being. Logotherapy has a concept of self-transcendence and we wrote of this in the previous chapter. Self-transcendence is the

It is important to understand that, as *Frankl says:* What matters is not the radius of your activities, but how well you fill its circle.

capacity to rise above who we are and 'to do the best thing', even though it may not be the easiest thing.

"What does the voice of self-transcendence say?" We need to add that to the three questions I already posed when considering a decision:

* What is best for me?

* What is best for others?

* What 'ought to be'?

* What does the voice of self-transcendence say?

In other words how good could I be? What am I called to do that is better than I ever thought was possible?

This is a story without an ending. My client and I parted company before he had made his final decision. I do know that what he decided was to tell his lover that they should not see each other now for three months as he had to make an important decision in life.

Marcia, I disagree that decisions can ever be reversed. **Each decision is unique.** I think what you mean is that we can rebuild and take meaningful decisions in the future. Yes, that is why guilt is such a positive thing if we see its potential in this way.

There will always be decisions we regret. But what we can do with our guilt about bad decisions, is to avoid making the same mistakes again.

Guilt in itself is a positive thing, if we treat it that way. It provides a guide post for how we could do things better next time.

A final thought …

There will always be challenges and failures. As you hint, Marcia, life will always have regrets.

Healthy Attitude
I always have a choice in life, even if it is only to choose the attitude I will take to unavoidable circumstance.

Unhealthy Attitude
Life is unfair. I do not deserve to be where I am right now. I may as well give up!

Healthy Attitude
Decisions based only on what is best for me will ultimately lack meaning.

Unhealthy Attitude
Look after 'number one'; no-one else will.

Healthy Attitude
Regrets about past decisions are guideposts to better decisions in the future.

Unhealthy Attitude
'Regrets, I've had a few, but then again, too few to mention.' (*From My Way*, sung by Frank Sinatra)

INTEGRITY

We are the sum total
of our actions.

I love this word! Integrity means wholeness, soundness, uprightness, honesty.

For me, this word means 'integrated':

> I do as I say I will do; I am who I say I am; I stand for what I believe in.

Each of us has and is a brand. Part of that brand is our integrity — just like a product or service!

Are we what we say we are? Do we do what we say we will do? Or are we one of those brands that simply does not live up to the advertising claims?

I have a number of friends who, every time I meet up with them, say the same thing—*I will call you*—and they never do! Perhaps they are just being polite and that is an easy way to say goodbye?

It can be very disillusioning when this happens to us, if we are really relying on these people to call. Men do this when they date! In the contemporary world of more equal dating, perhaps women do as well?

Lack of integrity leads not only to disillusionment but also to mistrust. We all probably have a mental list of people who have integrity and those who don't; those who will call if they say they will; those who will pay when they say they will; those who do what they say they will do — and the others. While 'the cheque in the mail' has been outdated by 24/7 online banking, there are still plenty of opportunities for us to show either our integrity or our lack of it!

Sadly, in public life we are constantly confronted by a lack of integrity — union leaders who steal from their own workers; politicians who lie to gain office and then find reasons for not doing the things they promised or who use their position to change laws to suit their own pockets and use their allowances for personal benefit; business leaders who steal from their companies; sports people who use drugs to win.

Whether or not these people end up in jail, they are largely discredited and their brand is tarnished. They are known to lack integrity and, in the end, they generally end up with the

Integrity is really the completed connection between our words and our actions.

consequences of their actions. They certainly lose any public trust.

Sometimes I hear people say, *so they do this, why shouldn't I?*

There are some very good reasons to work on our integrity and to consider it a key part of our personal brand — it's easier to sleep at night, it's easier to do business if you are trusted and it makes you feel better!

Any time I have let myself down in the integrity department, I have felt very disappointed with myself and I have never forgotten those times and actions. They stay with me and haunt me.

I remember distinctly being asked by my manager in my first corporate role, not to disclose my salary to anyone. Stupidly I allowed a very competitive fellow employee to glean that information from me. I still remember how bad I left when that manager called me in to his office. I knew exactly why I was there, there was no excuse. I had broken a clear agreement.

Integrity is really the completed connection between our words and our actions. Buddhists call this karma: *You reap what you sow.*

Coming from life in the country, I see a huge difference in general terms between the way country people and city people integrate their lives. Some years ago, I had an opportunity in the strangest way to reflect on this.

At that time I was CEO of Pola Cosmetics and, after many years of extremely hard work and often little return, I was finally starting to

'live the dream'. I had finally bought my own house and was dutifully paying the mortgage. As a CEO, I was being invited to interesting events and parties. But there was an event I had always wanted to go to because the idea fascinated me and it was called the Melbourne Cup of the Bush.

It was held in mountainous country in the north of Victoria, just two days before the real and glamorous Melbourne Cup. I persuaded a friend to drive with me, about a two-hour trip, and we arrived rather late to find that the main and toughest race of all had just finished. But there was more to come. Now this race was not quite like the Melbourne Cup, the Kentucky Derby or Royal Ascot. It was more like the traditional tribal horse events held in the hills of Afghanistan.

The actual track the horses ran was steep, dangerous and crossed rivers—just like cattlemen riding in the high country. I was intensely excited. While we were waiting for the next race, we visited one of the sponsor tent stores to look at the country gear.

My friend waited outside and I started a conversation with a young man who seemed to be buying the whole shop! When I commented on his shopping spree, he said in the broadest Australian drawl I had ever heard, *I am just claiming my prize for winning the main race* — the one we had just missed!

Of course, I became very curious about who he was, how he had become a mountain rider, how hard the race was and so on. He explained

that his win was made even more amazing by the fact that his horse had been knocked out during the race in the previous year and was to have been put down, but he had nursed it back to life!

The event became even more interesting when he invited us to join his other riding mates for a beer on the grass outside. This invitation presented quite a contrast to Melbourne Cup events featuring champagne and lobster! But we were at the event to join in and here we were, right in the middle of all these amazing young men from all over the state, who rode in these crazy, dangerous rides and then for fun went into the mountains mustering wild cattle on weekends. No clubbing for these guys!

My friend and I were entranced with their wild riding stories. When we told them that we also had been riders as children from the country, our very new friend asked if we would like to stay with him and spend a weekend riding. Too good to be true and, although we were both a bit hesitant about our riding skills in the mountains, we agreed and made a weekend time.

We returned to Melbourne and our friend, who was deaf in one ear due to a rabbit shooting accident, called to confirm the invitation. Yes, we accepted, and so had to fly to Albury, a city between Sydney and Melbourne, where he would meet us at the airport.

A couple of days before the weekend, my friend decided not to go. By this stage I was determined not to miss a one-off opportunity to go mountain riding but, without my friend, **I did feel more than just a slight hesitation!**

I had also given some thought to the accommodation. From what we had heard from the riders, this was not a glamorous life — most worked in basic labouring jobs to pay for their riding. I visited the local market and bought some delicious food. I also packed linen, as hitchhiking around the globe had taught me that, as long as the linen was clean, I could sleep anywhere!

Our friend met me at the airport. As we got into his ute, I noticed a sticker on the back with the letters 'NRNR'. I asked what this stood for. He looked a bit embarrassed and assured me it was not for me — I was quite glad about that when I hear the acronym was 'No Root No Ride'!

I checked that my mobile phone had power in case of emergency, held my breath and we started the three-hour drive to his farm, now greatly regretting that my friend was absent. As we drove, the country became poorer and poorer, with broken-down fences and houses with furniture on the verandas. I knew we would not be heading for five-star accommodation, but had no idea exactly how confronting the place this young man lived in would be.

The best way to describe the house we pulled up in front of (the worst I had seen on the drive so far!) is to say that the first thing I saw was a very large rat on the front gate.

Inside was unbelievable. No-one had cleaned this house for a very long time; no-one had picked up food scraps or papers. It was hard to walk across the floor—I dreaded the idea of the bathroom and bedroom. The amazing thing was that my new friend was

so welcoming and happy to show me his pad. This was the way he lived and this was what he was sharing with me — no frills, no flurry to tidy or clean up as this was his life. Even in all my travels in some of the poorest places on the planet, I had never seen such living!

The kitchen, the refrigerator, it just got worse. And as we walked out the back door to see his amazing horse that had recovered from the head injury, we stepped over a dead calf dragged to the back door intact—put there for the dogs to eat and they had started doing exactly that!

I lived in hope that the horse he adored may have at least lived in a nicer, cleaner place but was astonished to see his horse in a paddock full of junk and slush, equally uncared for.

My heavens! I was totally stuck for two nights with no motels in sight. But honestly, his openness and pride in what he had, would have prevented me from not staying. There was something so totally straight about him with no city guile or pretence, just 'this is me, this is my life and I would like to share with you'.

I slept those two nights in a room opposite the horse equipment room with a dirt floor but my own very clean sheets. I managed to keep my bathroom routine to a bare minimum and decided that I could do without showering for a couple of days.

We did go mountain riding as he had promised, and it was quite frightening going downhill on the horses. I have to admit that I walked my horse down anything too steep!

As we drove the long trek back to the airport, this young man told me that I was

Tips for Integrity:

✓ Make sure that you keep the promises you make.

✓ Reach out of your daily routine for new experiences and people.

✓ Treat everyone as equal, regardless of circumstance.

✓ Say what you mean and mean what you say.

✓ Identify and beware of spin!

welcome any time for a weekend. As I reflected on his guileless hospitality, I realised that he had shown me his life exactly as it was and had no hesitation in sharing his home. **He was exactly who he said he was; he lived in the only way he knew and was prepared to share what he had.**

That weekend reminded me of some of my very happy experiences as a back packer, being offered hospitality by people who had warmly opened their homes and hearts, despite their poverty.

When I arrived back at my business later that day, I felt an incredible sense of humility and an increased consciousness about the need to be more myself and more careful about how integrated my words and actions were.

No, I did not go back for a repeat weekend. But the lesson has remained with me and I have often reflected on the value of knowing totally open, honest, guileless people in a world so often caught up in spin!

Integrity and conscience

Marcia,

What does your concept of integrity mean for logotherapy? You mention first that each of us a 'brand'. Yes, I agree, each person is different and what we each contribute to or take from this world will be different. **This is the logotherapy concept of uniqueness, one of the pathways to finding meaning in life.** I will expand on this in our next chapter. For the moment stay with the concept of conscience because conscience is not just tied, but literally welded to integrity.

You suggest that there have been times when you may have let yourself down in the 'integrity department' and relate this to karma, the idea that 'you reap what you sow.' Yes, but this is not always so in a material sense – only in your deepest heart. There are many examples of people who lack integrity but make a fortune! However, I believe that somewhere, at some stage of life, they will question themselves deeply about their life. That is conscience.

"What about the dictators, the abusers, those who seem evil to their very core?" I hear you ask. Surely they put their conscience to sleep? Anaesthetise their conscience if you like.

Frankl was asked that very question about those who committed such horrors in the concentration camps. He was clear that we can never anaesthetise our conscience. What human beings can do and what they actually do is to anaesthetise themselves against their conscience; that is to resolve to take no notice of it. But it is still ticking; it does not go away.

Frankl believed that Hitler could never have been what he was unless he suppressed his conscience. That is, Frankl believed his conscience was still there but was simply put into the background without its questions being allowed to surface. We will come back to this later.

This is why I try to help clients find a positive way to view personal failures. It is difficult to convince ourselves sometimes, but guilt is a very positive thing. Yes, for if we have guilt then our conscience is communicating with us!

How should we handle guilt? Step one of course, is to acknowledge that we could have been a better person. Conscience is telling you that quite clearly. But as I pointed out when talking about decisions, the only way forward is what you decide to do now. You cannot reverse the past. What you can do is to resolve to do it differently now.

Our conscience is intuitive. It is the intuitive capacity to find meaning in any situation. This explains why you say you sleep better at night when you are trusted in your business dealings — it makes you feel better!

At a deeper level you have discerned a meaning in your dealings with others that provides you with a settled and a 'good' conscience. That you were 'trusted' and lived up to the trust shows that you did the best by all concerned, not simply for yourself. That decision provided the meaning. Remember our decision making process? You focussed on "what is best for others" and "what ought to be" as you worked on your business dealings. Of course you wanted "what is best for me" as part of that, after all a business has to make a profit! But it was not the sole consideration.

Conscience is that small inner voice that tells us whether our chosen path is meaningful. Intuitive conscience reflects our values. Much of intuitive conscience is built from the values we inherited from the family that nurtured us and the society in which we grew up. That is why those early years are so important.

Certainly the values that guide our conscience and meaningful decisions are largely inherited. They tend to guide our intuitive conscience.

But if values are nurtured at a young age, can we overcome what might be considered a difficult or abusive childhood? Yes, not just because we have control over our decisions right now, but because that inner voice of conscience tells us what is best. We may have had to observe "family" and "love" from the outside rather than experience it ourselves in the way each child should, but we will learn our own values from that, rejecting past negative experience and resolving to forge a different life path.

Our conscience is *intuitive.* It is the intuitive capacity to find meaning in any situation.

You see, conscience can also be creative. Sometimes we stand against the tide. The personal value and meaning of today, expressed by but a few, perhaps in protest against the majority, can become the universal value of humanity tomorrow. That is the creativity of conscience.

Some values belong to each person, built over time and through life-experience. If this did not happen, values would never change across the generations.

So be true to your values? Is that all it takes? Not really, because values that guide every decision are not necessarily simple to balance against each other. Values can be in conflict. The meaning of what we choose to do is unique.

That may sound simple enough, but it definitely is not. One client had been brought up with a very strict moral code at home. Hence,

he was in some trauma when he decided that, to be true to himself, he had to reveal to his parents that he was in fact gay. In his heart he was certain they would simply reject him. It would probably be his last face-to-face encounter he thought.

No doubt the parents also wrestled with their own demons when confronted with this. They rejected same-sex attraction as not only unnatural but against a divine law. Yet, this was their son.

I am happy to tell you that he was embraced by them for who he is and supported as a son, no matter what conflicting values they had as parents. This decision of acceptance had a unique meaning.

We have to make our way along life's rocky pathway without always being sure footed. Is it possible to follow one's conscience, to take meaningful decisions and directions, without

being certain that these meaningful directions are indeed for the best, because we have a conflict of values? Yet we must decide, we must move forward and the decision we take will have a unique meaning.

Gordon Allport, Professor of Psychology at Harvard who sponsored Frankl's original trips to the United States, puts it this way: "It is possible to be half sure and wholehearted". In other words, it is possible to be uncertain and yet realise the imperative of having to choose a path and take a firm decision. Choosing a responsible and meaningful direction in this way requires integrity.

Possibly, on reflection and after the event, we may conclude that the path we chose was not for the best. In that case we must take responsibility for our actions, for after all we have no choice but to do so. **The real task is then to discern the next step in life's journey, resolving not to make the same mistake again.**

It is important in all this to understand that the therapist is always helping a client to discern and define their own meaning. It is not ethical, nor indeed possible, to impose meanings on another person. I can help you discern a pathway that you perceive to provide meaning, but I cannot walk with you along it.

Conscience will always be there. We will always question whether the paths we take, the paths we choose, are meaningful. Ultimately human beings cannot avoid this.

Remember what we said earlier about anaesthesia of the conscience.

The capacity to suppress our conscience explains your comment on public life and the lack of integrity of those who use their position in society to line their own pockets, rather than benefit those they are supposed to serve. In my experience, most people I meet and certainly clients who seek help, will eventually wrestle with conscience, even if it has been suppressed. At some time, usually later in life, they will go through their own crisis of Integrity.

I am reminded of that wonderful line from *A Man For All Seasons* when Thomas More speaks about his refusal to take the oath required by the Act of Succession and demanded by the king:

"When a man takes an oath, he is holding himself like water in the palm of his hands, and if he opens his fingers then, he can never hope to find himself again."

Healthy Attitude:
Values can be in conflict, so taking meaningful decisions can be a struggle.

Unhealthy Attitude:
Decisions are good or bad, there is no in between.

Healthy Attitude:
If my intuition tells me this is wrong, listen. Conscience will not go away.

Unhealthy Attitude:
Go with the flow. Everyone else is doing it, so why not me?

Healthy Attitude:
A few people prepared to stand up for their beliefs today can make a difference tomorrow.

Unhealthy Attitude:
I can make no difference, so just let it be and say nothing.

uniqueness

Do not wish to be anything
but what you are and
try to be that perfectly.

My father, who died some years ago, had many sayings which I have never forgotten (the power of parenting!). One of his favourites and mine was: **"Always do your best".**

He was always humming that old refrain from a well-known song: *Do what you do do well.*

This was my guiding light through my school years and even in boarding school, far from my father's care. I could hear his voice on the sports field and in the classroom. This simple saying drove me and I always felt good about myself when I did my best — even if my best was not always successful!

I loved sport and vowed to be in all the school teams apart from swimming (as a country girl I had never been taught to swim) and this mantra drove me. As I quickly gained a reputation in my new city boarding school as an all-round sports-girl, I was invited to join the school swimming team without even trying out. No matter how much I tried to persuade the school swimming captain that I could barely keep my head above water, she put me in the team. Horror of horrors, I could not even dive! I was in a state of panic, but nothing would dissuade her.

As I lined up on the blocks, the whistle blew and I jumped into the water as my opposition dived in. I popped up to the surface to see sprays of freestyle water way ahead of me. I floundered and performed something between a dog paddle and freestyle. I felt utterly humiliated but did my best to get to the end of the pool. The only thing that saved me from total shame in front of the whole senior school was that I had done my best. Of course, the swimming captain did not quite see it that way — she could not comprehend that a girl from a farm far from swimming pools, lakes and the ocean had never been taught to swim!

We often see people with great talent squander it and equally we see people living every day at their best. They do not always succeed, but they can rest easy in the knowledge that they did their best.

In this area, my father was a wonderful role model. He always gave his best to his family and his farm — his two great loves. That powerful role model has never left me. In the course of always trying to doing my best, I sometimes feel frustrated when I don't succeed at whatever I have taken on. But I always feel great when I know that I have done all I could.

I often meet with and see people who have given up on doing their best. They have lost that zest, that inner fire. Near enough has become good enough.

Many western societies with generous welfare schemes seem to have fostered a 'near enough' culture. Any system that disables people from achieving their best is failing to do the best by the very people who need that motivation. In Australia, we seem to be cultivating a victim mentality that is counterproductive to encouraging people to do their best.

Some of our Olympians, who had the privilege of representing Australia in the

2012 Olympic Games held in London, adopted that attitude and apparently drank and partied before their events. There is no doubt that this prevented them from doing their best. With privilege comes the responsibility of performing at one's highest level. Not only did this group of Olympians let their country and its taxpayers down, they prevented others who did not make the team from having that opportunity.

We sometimes feel that, with so many wars and massacres happening in many parts of the world, things can't ever have been worse. So what difference can we as individuals make?

I think we need to get some perspective on this and consider the fact that, at the very same time as all these incredibly distressing things are happening — massacres in the Middle East; human slavery in some dark regions of the African continent; child sex abuse in all parts of the world; the degradation of women in many cultures—mankind has never achieved so much:

* true democracy in many parts of the world

* equality of opportunity for men and women

* greater awareness of our environment and protection of endangered species

* cures for diseases that previously killed millions

* people performing all sorts of humanitarian and philanthropic acts daily

I am totally in awe of people who give their best at whatever they do; they are the ones who have the power to change the world. I think of the work of Nelson Mandela, Indira Ghandi, Aung San Suu Kyi, medical researchers, volunteers and the list goes on. Actually, I admire those people who have given their best even in positions that some may look down on. There is something uplifting when you hear people say I love what I do and I always do my best.

Unfortunately, sometimes people have evil intentions behind doing their best. I think of the Nazi intent to rid Europe of Jews and the determination of Pol Pot to destroy his fellow countrymen. The list of such people is also long and exhaustive. These evil beings sadly are not unique and require those with integrity to speak up and stand up.

Besides doing our best, we need to have principles that enable us to ensure our best efforts are both self-fulfilling and beneficial to the community and the planet. Each of us is unique and has the capacity to use our uniqueness to make the planet a better place.

Imagine a world where everyone was committed to the best use of their talents in this way! Imagine if each of us woke up every day determined to do our best!

Recently, Rupert Murdoch used words to this effect:

"The most moral thing you can do for someone is help them be their best".

Tips for Uniqueness:

✓ Commit to making the most of each day by doing your best at the task at hand.

✓ Work out the most powerful way you can impact on the people and world around you and do it.

✓ Accept that near enough is not good enough!

✓ Acknowledge and encourage others to do their best.

You Live Life Only Once – Use It Well

Marcia,

Imagine what the world might be like if 'always do your best' was the slogan by which all of us lived. There would still be problems, however, because how to interpret "doing your best" is the issue. Frankl admits in the last section of *Man's Search for Meaning*:

> The world is in a bad state, but everything will become still worse unless each of us does his best ... Since Auschwitz we know what man is capable of. And since Hiroshima we know what is at stake.'

Logotherapy always operates in the dimension of the human 'essence' or 'spirit'. As long as we interpret 'doing your best' as achieving in a material sense, or even achieving intellectually, we run the risk of only hearing part of the message of this powerful approach to life and therapy. **So 'doing your best' refers to the attitude we take to what is happening in our life.** We are always capable of rising above even the most difficult circumstance.

An exercise I sometimes do with clients is to have them answer some simple questions. I ask those in plain type first, then pose those in italics – they are the tough ones, but the most important.

When and where were you born?

Was this an accident? What were you born for at that time and place?

How many years have you lived?

What have you survived for? What will you do with your future life now?

How many schools have you attended?

Was this an accident or were you meant to be there?

We could go on with questions such as these – and you could add your own questions beneath each.

When did you leave school?

How many siblings do you have?

Why were you not born into an African tribe or in Mongolia or Patagonia? (Careful of this one if your client is actually African etc.!) Of course there is no answer to the "accident" question. The real point here is to emphasise the real uniqueness of the person.

Uniqueness is a very demanding concept if we take it seriously. Not only are we living each day in a way that can never be repeated, we come into contact each day with others whose life is also unique. Our short encounter with them can be a positive or negative experience. **Try as we might to live up to our ideals, most of us will never really know the result our actions have on others.**

One classic story, not a cheerful one, is the accidental way in which World War I began. Many know its origins lie in the assassination of Archduke Franz Ferdinand in Sarajevo. Few remember the assassin, Gavrilo Princip. Fewer still know that Princip was only one of many potential assassins on the street that day, and that they all decided to give up and go home when the Duke's motorcade was involved in an accident and turned back. The show was over, they would have to wait for another day to display their revolutionary fervour!

However, Princip did not go directly home but stopped off for coffee and a sandwich. It was only later that day that the Duke decided to visit the hospital where the accident victims had been taken. So the motorcade set out again, this time on a slightly different route. During the trip the driver took a wrong turn and decided to reverse and so the Archduke's car stopped, right across from Princip's coffee house! It was only then that Princip, quite accidentally as it turned out, was in the right place at the right time to fire the shot that began a war and indirectly killed millions.

We can never know the end result of what we do. **What we can do is to act with integrity by following our conscience.** Then the result is more likely to be positive for a greater number.

I am reminded of one of my clients who is afflicted with severe depression. She can become very introspective and has some very dark moments. However she once saved a colleague from suicide, and when we meet and she is in this dark place I remind her about this.

She did not know she was saving a life at the time. It was only much later that the girl thanked her for taking the time to sit and talk because, on that very day, she was ready to go out and end her life. But having someone who was interested enough to stop and take the time to talk changed her direction. I remind my client of this when she becomes depressed about her own life and achievements. Simply reflecting on what is unique about our life and what we have achieved is therapeutic, if only we fully realise how irreplaceable we really are.

Logotherapy always operates in the dimension of the human 'essence' or 'spirit'.

If we fully understand that each of us is unique then understanding that we are challenged to take meaning-filled decisions is an easy and reasonable step. The alternative is to conclude that life has no meaning. In that case there is little point in protecting it or prolonging it. However, something in the makeup of human beings rejects that notion.

We do mourn over the tragic loss of life in a plane crash, even without knowing personally any of the victims.

The discovery of the human genome and DNA has done us a wonderful service. It proves beyond doubt that each person is uniquely constructed. Sometimes discoveries in the physical are a great assistance to other human dimensions.

There will never be another person anything like us in this world and the whole DNA identification process depends upon this. Fingerprints were a first step of course, but a comparatively weak way to convince us of the uniqueness of each person. DNA is absolute.

However, uniqueness is a heavy burden to carry. If we really believe we are unique,

it places on our shoulders a profound responsibility. Since there can only be one of us, we have some important choices to make.

We can decide to be the best person we can possibly become, or we can decide to acquiesce in being something less than that.

We can realise that each person we meet is unique and hence our encounter with that person, the opportunity to touch their lives and allow them to touch our own, may come only once.

This web of intertwined relationships with others means that we can never really know the effect of what we have done. Another of my clients suffers from such severe depressive bouts and anxiety that he is unable to work anymore. How does his fairly solitary existence make any difference to this world?

When he is really "down" I remind him of a moment of personal pride in his life. He once saved a little girl from drowning. He did not know her, he did not know the family, but he could swim, the mother was distraught on the beach unable to do anything, and he swam out and saved her life. Sometimes, when he has been depressed and life seemed to have no meaning, I have asked him:

"I wonder what that little girl you saved is doing now?"

"If saving that one person from drowning was the only significant event you can name, would your life have been worthwhile?"

My answer to the first question is: "We can never know". That is life's mystery. What we can know is that my wonderful client gave that young person a chance to continue the most important thing for any person: life.

Hence my answer to the second question, and my client has the same answer, is: "Undoubtedly yes".

As Frankl says: "One moment can retrospectively flood an entire life with meaning".

No-one can ever know if their hour, their unique personal challenge, is to arrive tomorrow.

It is only when we direct ourselves to something or someone other than ourselves (be it a meaning to fulfil, a cause to support or another human being to encounter), that we are able to forget ourselves and rise above what we ever thought we could be. I have never worked with a client that has not actually done this at some time in life. I have met many who need to be reminded of that event and have it treasured for what it is, the taking a very human positive attitude to life itself.

You see, there are so many examples in this world where people choose to be 'true to themselves' to 'pursue happiness' and they miss the point that this requires self-transcendence. This is the capacity to take an attitude that responds to life's challenge and in that way to rise above current circumstance.

The mistake we make is to take the ordinary human being as only a mixture of the physical and the psychological. However **we have a particular human quality that allows us to rise above the ordinary and take a stand.**

Frankl believed there are two 'races' of people in this world and only two. First is the 'race' of the decent. Opposed to this is the 'race' of the indecent. Life challenges us to join the first race, which runs across gender and ethnic divides.

The first task is to make a difference in ourselves: to harness our existence. Perhaps those who do so will always be a minority — but a significant minority which can make a difference in this world.

Religions have often taught that each person is a unique creation of a supreme being. **As logotherapists we simply believe that each person has a unique meaning to fulfil and to discover in this world.**

Discovering our own meaning then connects with an ultimate meaning, whatever form that takes.

The capacity to rise above the self, to transcend even the most difficult obstacles, is a particular human capacity that provides us with a direction and challenge for life.

Rabbi Hillel once said to his students:

If I don't do it, who will do it? If I don't do it now, when will I do it? And if I do it only for myself, then who am I?

Healthy Attitude:
To be all I can be I must focus outwards and aspire to a meaning beyond myself.

Unhealthy Attitude:
To be true to myself and find happiness is the most important value in life.

Healthy Attitude:
I am unique and all I do is important in this world.

Unhealthy Attitude:
It matters little what I do; I am a mere pawn in a larger game.

Healthy Attitude:
I may never know the effect I have had on others. Each encounter is important and unique.

Unhealthy Attitude:
Everyone makes their own way in life. I am not responsible for them; they are not responsible for me.

LEARNING

You cannot discover new oceans,
unless you have the
courage to lose sight of the shore.

Green and growing — that is such a great way to live life!

If we are open to learning, every day something happens that teaches us something about ourselves and others. We can either feel frustrated that we don't know more, or excited by the opportunity of learning more.

I had my lesson about the need for daily learning when, after eleven years of university degrees both full and part-time, I met the man who taught me about business and how to deal with life challenges. He had to leave school when he was fourteen, as his parents could no longer afford his train fare. He was the man who started me on my Pola business life; in one month I learnt more about myself, my fears, my shortcomings and my ability than I had learnt in all those years at university.

Sure, I learnt some great theoretical and thought-provoking facts in those eleven years, but I did not learn about the importance of such things as the need to take risks, test my skills, try to persuade others, or confront my fears.

He, of course, had had to do this to survive. For my part, I had lived a rather enclosed life in boarding school, university, teaching and then the corporate world. All great places to be, until you are put to the test of life!

Fortunately, my love of learning (as evidenced by my addiction to accumulating degrees) now had to be put to the test as I faced the reality of a marriage breakdown, financial challenges and a whole new business life, consequently my whole focus changed to learning about business and personal survival.

There is nothing like a major hiccup in life to make one learn. Pity we have to have that to learn survival skills.

I remember once seeing a very good illustration of the need for learning.

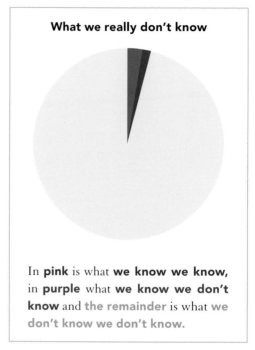

What we really don't know

In **pink** is what **we know we know,** in **purple** what **we know we don't know** and the remainder is what we don't know we don't know.

I think the digital age has confronted us with the reality of how little we know and how much we don't know.

In my adult life, we have moved from

If we are open to learning, every day something happens that teaches us something about ourselves and others.

typewriters to computers to tablets; from telegrams (remember the ones always read out at weddings!) to telexes, to faxes, to emails to Facebook; and from newspapers to TV to tablets.

So where lies the future? What genius is going to change our lives again? And how?

We can't all be Steve Jobs, whose curious and restless mind gave us products that have changed the way millions of people absorb information and communicate with each other, but we can be open to the ideas of these incredible people at the forefront of change. Having an open learning attitude to life gives us the confidence to take on new challenges. But it also keeps us nicely humble, knowing that so rapidly we can be out of our depth and needing to learn all over again.

Of course, some things never change, such as basic human values and the way we treat and communicate with each other. But when it comes to the way we connect and the way we absorb information, it seems that we need to be learning something new every day!

I believe that whatever the mode of connection, **we get the best results in life and business if politeness and respect are maintained in that communication.**

Age does not prevent us from learning. In fact, as we get older, the importance of learning becomes greater and so our world gets bigger and more exciting. We have the experience to sift discerningly through new ideas and take the best.

There is another great value in believing in the importance of learning: it keeps you feeling young. One of my many ongoing daily challenges is around the digital world; trying to get the most from it, from both a business and personal perspective.

Every day I open my laptop and look at my iPhone or iPad. I am distinctly reminded of the need to learn more about how these seemingly complicated tools work. Equally, when it comes to understanding people and the world around us, there is something new to take on board every day.

Sometimes as adults, we feel that we have to fake knowledge to make ourselves seem more important. This strategy can sometimes work for us, my first public speaking experiences required that I sometimes spoke more confidently than I felt! Most times it is better to admit a lack of understanding about an issue and fill that gap as quickly as possible.

I have learnt many lessons around this, particularly in business. I have found that it is always better to ask questions when we don't understand something, rather than pretend that we do!

Someone once said to me: *The quality of your life is related to the quality of your questions.* I have noticed that, when people ask questions, it is often a relief to those around them who were not brave enough to show their hand.

We often find the things we don't understand are equally not understood by others!

Tips for Learning:

✓ Be prepared to ask questions, even if no-one else is.

✓ Make a commitment to learn something new each day.

✓ At the end of each day or week, think about what you have learnt.

✓ See learning as a positive challenge, not a frustration.

Logotherapy is Not a Cure for Life

Marcia,

Learning from life experience is a central theme that I often explore with clients.

Most therapeutic approaches aim to divert the client's mind away from disturbed or disturbing experiences, and this is appropriate, but in the long term it will not be enough. Once the disturbing issue, be it anxiety, depression, addiction or something else is brought under control, we are still left to face life itself. We may be "cured" of our most severe symptoms, but there is no "cure" for life.

Stabilising the patient's symptoms is a laudable aim for medicine and therapy. A state of equilibrium, curing the presenting issue, may be possible in the physical and the psychological dimensions, but not in our inner selves. (Frankl often took issue with the concept of what is called homeostasis, as it refers to a state of inner equilibrium)[5]. Our broken ankle is set and it heals, possibly not to what it was, but at least it is now usable again. Our anxiety reaction to dogs is overcome by reason and exposure to the problem – dogs! We realise it is illogical to fear every dog, so we train

ourselves to first of all decide if this particular canine is a danger. Then we either take evasive action or disregard our first response.

Equilibrium, or "cure", is not possible nor even desirable in life itself. Remember, **logotherapy is about coping with life, so it is bigger than the physical or psychological.** It is about the real depth of the person. The real, particular "human" qualities we all have within us.

A lack of tension in life, were it even possible, will lead to boredom, frustration and a lack of direction. Life has to have a certain degree of challenge and tension to be healthy. That is why the concept of **learning is important.**

We can look at each failure and success in life, and both will be there in some ways, to provide a lesson in what might have been done differently and hence an opportunity to learn. On the other hand, we can simply rejoice in the success phase of life and avoid accepting the failures.

If we focus only on our successes then we learn little and possibly limit our chances of future success. A focus only on our failures,

if taken to extremes, can lead to significant disorders of the human spirit. No success is perfect, no failure absolute. We can have a success with no meaning, which is why seemingly successful people can take their own lives. Deep down their quest was for meaning and it was never found.

On the other hand **a failure can be the result of a very meaning-filled initiative.** Crisis call centres sometimes have failures, the caller gives up and ends their life. Yet would anyone dispute that the provision of a service to the caller, the fact that the last voice that caller heard was from someone who expressed concern and care, was not meaningful in its own right?

It is a disorder of the spirit not to welcome and acknowledge the necessary tensions in life. It can express itself as either a physical or a psychological symptom, but it remains a disorder of the spirit — a failure to properly engage with life.

I once worked with a client who had a tendency to freeze the muscles down one side of the body when he became anxious. He could look paralysed on the right side, if there was a severe anxiety attack. Emotionally, his anxiety could then express itself as anger. He came to me because of a threat of retrenchment from work. This threat seemed to attack his last citadel of personhood, his job.

His marriage had been a 'disaster' from his own description of it. Since coming together and immigrating to Australia, he had never found a job that really extended him or built upon his real talent.

His identity centred on his job and success here. There had been prestige in what he had done at work before coming to a new country. There was little prestige in a lower level role, and now even that was under threat. Yet he was proud of his children and what they had achieved. We spoke for hours about the current job and the stupidity of management, but after a time we always were able to move to the family and what he really treasured – his

children. Once he focused on the victories he had achieved in life, rather than on its defeats, his anxiety subsided.

The problems of his marriage were still there, the problem in his job remained, but they no longer mattered. What he could see was the good. What he was able to accept was the reality. I can remember him saying to me when I asked about the job and the potential redundancy after quite a few sessions together, "It's not important anymore." He had learned to cope with life itself.

You see, learning is something we can take from every life experience. On the other hand, we can choose to see the negative experiences only as defeats. So, I take your point. Taking on new challenges is great. However, remaining humble and realising that we can rapidly get out of our depth, is also something we may need to address.

Logotherapy, because it operates at the spiritual or 'core' of the human being, provides deep learning about life itself and how we need to approach its challenges. Many of these learnings are outlined in Frankl's original best-selling book *Man's Search for Meaning*.

First is **acceptance of reality.** Prisoners taken into the concentration camps were first stripped naked and left with nothing. To realise that life can so quickly have all possessions, achievements, degrees and status taken away is a real challenge to our acceptance of reality. Victims of major accidents often face this – and with help can learn again to cope with what life now challenges them to be.

Could you face this? None of us knows how we would respond, but we have the capacity within us to respond and rise up from tragedy.

The learning for those in the concentration camps, particularly for those with a medical background, was about the human capacity to respond to any challenge. For instance, the medical textbooks said that the human being needs a certain amount of sleep in order to operate and that there are some things that we cannot live without. Maslow's much quoted *Hierarchy of Needs* is based on this.

Frankl disputes this. The concentration camp prisoners very quickly realised that their sleeping conditions and their living conditions were such that simply surviving each day was an achievement. Yet they were able to rise above that, knowing that they faced almost certain death. They kept going because survival itself was important.

Their loved ones had been taken from them and so a further learning was that love itself goes far beyond the physical person that we love. Its deepest meaning is in the spiritual presence; whether the person is physically present or not is not the most important issue. It is the memories and the understandings we share, and the capacity to have the other present in our own imagination. These are the deepest parts of love.

Then there was the attitude to fate itself. The prisoners had no power over anything and knew that fate must take its course. Whether they survived or not would be a matter of fate and accident. The decision about their future would be taken by someone else. It mattered

little who was loaded on to the transport to go to the gas chamber, as long as the numbers were met. Thus, whether you survived or not was a matter of where you stood in the line.

Yet they were not powerless. **They could choose how they would respond to their situation.** Even when life seemed hopeless, the choice was still there to hold one's head high or dissolve into despair. As Frankl says: "We who survived know that the best of us did not come back".

Translated into logotherapy terms, what each of us must learn about life is that it is not a question of what we expect from life, but rather that **we are always challenged to answer the question of what life expects from us** — now, today, in whatever challenges and questions it poses. We only hope they are not as severe as those posed to Frankl and his colleagues.

So the most profound learning about life is that, even under the most difficult circumstances, the human being is capable of taking an attitude. Of standing up and being counted and using what we call 'the defiant power of the human spirit' to be able to cope.

Your reflection on learning reminded me of a collective learning that is often part of our society today. It is a learned meaninglessness. This is what Frankl calls 'the existential vacuum'.

The image of a "vacuum" implies a life is lived without meaning and eventually even without the energy to search for meaningful activities. So we search for the wrong things — happiness, avoidance of pain and suffering, the 'good life' however we conceive it. All of these things are *cul de sacs* on life's journey. Such things as happiness have to result from meaningful activity and cannot be pursued as an end. Suffering should be avoided wherever possible, but some suffering is inevitable and our response must be to find the meaning in it: to learn from it.

Many of the learnings above, which are core to logotherapy, are quite readily understood by 'the man in the street'. Intuitively, we know what we must do in difficult circumstances and we know how to recover. However, increasingly it seems that we are being told we have a right to be happy, satisfied and comfortable. When any of these things are taken away or challenged, it is our attitude to life that must then see us through.

Healthy Attitude:
Each day I try to respond to what life asks of me now, today, where I am.

Unhealthy Attitude:
I keep asking myself what I want from this life.

Healthy Attitude:
Pain and suffering are inevitable in life. It is how we respond that makes the difference.

Unhealthy Attitude:
Negative experiences, failures and suffering are to be avoided at all costs.

Healthy Attitude:
A healthy tension is an important and inevitable part of living.

Unhealthy Attitude:
I seek for a life without tension. I long for peace.

BALANCE

Never let yesterday
take up too much of today.

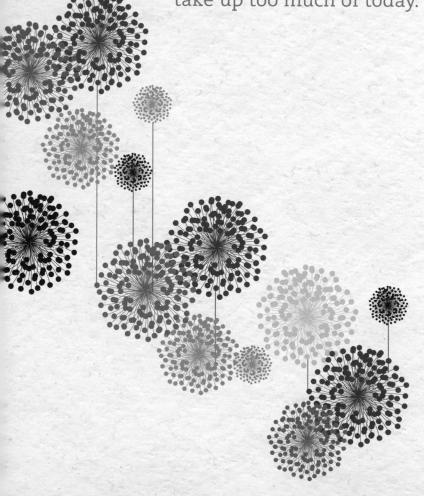

Finding balance in our lives is valuable in many ways. If we are always focussed on the past, we can never move forward, if we only think of the future, we will not live consciously today, if we only think of today, we fail to plan for the future.

We need to find balance between the past, present and future and equally find a balance in our own internal makeup.

Just as businesses look at their balance sheet we can do a personal balance sheet to test this balance in our lives. I like to put my life into four categories when I do my personal balance sheet.

* Spiritual

* Physical

* Emotional

* Financial

I find it really helpful to constantly assess how I am doing in these key areas of my life. If we pay attention to all four of them, it can give us great comfort. To focus simply on one of these areas leads to imbalance and dissatisfaction — just as focussing on the one part of our timeline, past, present or future, will lead to imbalance.

By spiritual life, I am not referring to any particular religion. In fact, I was brought up in a strict Catholic environment but I have totally rejected all but the basic Christian values. While there may be many great people who are capable of giving amazing spiritual leadership across a number of religions, I recognise that organised religion has been and continues to be the cause of most wars, oppression, abuse of individuals and abuse of power. As a woman, my perception is that most religions have oppressed women throughout history and some continue to do that today.

By spiritual, I really mean something very personal—the state of one's soul. The inner fire. That voice within us. That essence that defines us. It is that part of us over which no-one else has. It is the very core of our being. **Our spiritual life needs nourishing, encouraging and nurturing.**

For me, that nurture comes from finding people and places that enable my spirit to soar. Those places can be a deserted beach, an amazing sunset, an historical site; those people can include a wonderful friend who inspires and encourages, powerful words, uplifting human behaviour. Those people can also be individuals who are doing great things on the planet or simply people whose spirit is good! I am inspired by researchers who spend their lives looking for a tiny bug; athletes whose dedication and behaviour is uplifting to the human spirit; philanthropists who do great things for others; and people who share their hard-earned wealth. I try to focus on these people, rather than the overblown celebrities and the seriously bad people on the planet.

Unfortunately, the media tends to focus on the bad rather than the good, so it is easy for us to feel disillusioned with the world around us. The media, of course, has to sell its stories and it is true that human curiosity may

make stories about bad people more sellable. However, I believe that most people are trying to do the right thing. Yes, there is an evil minority but, in fair societies, these people are eventually punished.

I remember a really wonderful piece of advice about the sort of pervasive negative news that we are bombarded with every day:

Worry only about the things you can do something about and do something about them!

Essentially, our spirit soars when we have a good hard look at the bright, shining, uplifting parts of life. They are there for us all to see and benefit from.

Searching for the source of spiritual contentment is a very worthwhile journey. If we are not conscious of the need to nurture this part of our life, we may live in a permanent state of discontent. For some of us, it may mean journeying to gurus in foreign countries but if we look closely at life around us we may realise that we are surrounded by the natural environment (even in a big city), people, actions and ideas that can enhance our spiritual contentment.

Many years ago, initially through a business situation, I met a friend who I consider to be a soul mate — someone who has the uncanny knack of contacting me and encouraging me whenever there is a challenge, crisis or adventure looming.

Several years ago, I was completely exhausted from the endless pace of business. My doctor suggested that I try some anti-depressants. I agreed and took home a box of tablets ready to make an immediate start, even though I felt a little disconcerted by the ease of access to this pharmaceutical crutch. As I drove around the corner to my house, my friend Greg was waiting at the gate. We had agreed to meet that evening and I had simply forgotten our arrangement. Once again his timing was perfect. It did not take long for him to encourage me to look at the reasons I was considering anti-depressants and what I could do instead of relying on pharmaceuticals.

By the time he left we had talked, laughed and put the exhaustion I was feeling in perspective. Yes, I was exhausted. Yes, I did need to focus on the great things in my life, stress less about the small issues and celebrate the wonderful things — including having friends like this remarkable and inspiring man.

Of course, **it's hard to feel good about yourself when your physical self is not in good shape.**

How many books, websites or gurus do we need to read and listen to, to believe in the importance of being healthy? Our body is the fabulous thing that holds us together, transports us around and presents us to the world!

Our body has so many important roles and yet we have a largely self-imposed obesity crisis in the western world. This crisis has reached a stage where recently a man was not allowed to travel by aeroplane because of his enormous weight.

Deepak Chopra says:

"Every living cell in your body is eavesdropping on your mind."

If we tell ourselves that our body deserves respect, we will treat it with respect. If we think our body does not matter, then we are well on the way to overeating, obesity and all the health problems that result.

In conjunction with eating is the role that exercise plays in keeping us fit. I am sure that at this time in the history of the western world, more money is spent on gyms, exercise machines and health retreats than ever before. Yet obesity is in plague proportions in these countries. It seems that the richer we get, the fatter we get!

It is also said that today, in the western world, we are doing about one-tenth the exercise of people who lived a hundred years ago. Let's think about it: we get up, go to work by car, bus or train, sit all day, then come home and watch TV. At weekends we go and watch someone else playing sport. We could all live like this if we don't value the role of exercise!

Every day, I start out with physical exercise. This ensures that I don't have an excuse not to exercise later in the day. The value I get from this is the reassurance that I still have the discipline to do it; the great way my body feels after exercising; and the opportunity to see the sunrise, listen to birds (even in the middle of the city) and generally feel grateful for another great day on the planet!

I sometimes go to a gym but really treat my life like a daily workout: I vacuum my house, look after my garden and wash my own car. I simply can't see the point of paying gym fees when we can use our own houses or apartments as live-in gyms!

The emotional part of life can be the toughest. Divorce and the inability to have children may seem to be very debilitating but actually there is life beyond both these challenges.

I have noticed there are plenty of young people in the world seeking mentoring and support. I feel lucky to have some of these young people discuss their challenges with me and ask for advice. I may even have more proximity to them than I might have had with children of my own.

I feel the need to seek out supportive and positive people: they are the ones who give me emotional support and, in turn, I find that I am often giving out that same support to others. I notice that these sets of people are not the same. But both the giving and the getting are equally rewarding and nurturing.

Many years ago a friend of mine, a global traveller and business man, made a statement that I questioned at the time:

"There are two types of people in the world— givers and takers."

To find emotional balance and satisfaction we need to be a giver and avoid the takers!

The financial part of our lives is the fourth part to assess and consider. Robert Kiyosaki summed it up:

"There is nothing charming about poverty."

We all have different attitudes and values around avoiding poverty. We do have a responsibility to ourselves to protect our financial lives and, as this is the area where the greatest sharks lie, we need eternal vigilance!

My lessons around money are to not hand over this responsibility without very careful consideration. I include in this spouses, advisors — actually anyone at all. We cannot let others run this part of our lives without watching their efforts carefully and making sure they are operating in our best interests.

It seems to me that in this part of life we need to make smart, sensible decisions based on all the knowledge we can get. We need to read, learn and keep up-to-date with what is happening in the financial world. Yes, this can be challenging. Fortunately, there are some basic rules around money that can put a safeguard around our financial health:

✳ We need to know our own risk appetite.

✳ We need to spend less than we earn.

✳ We should — once again to quote Robert Kiyosaki — "Borrow only for assets or cash flow!"

✳ We should separate our needs from our wants and spend on needs first.

✳ We should understand that, in our affluent western world, we can never have enough of what we don't need!

Balancing All Human Dimensions

Marcia,

Your "personal balance sheet" concerns me. I simply can't agree with rating 'finance' or any other material need on the same level as the spiritual, physical and emotional. My work as a therapist concentrates on **combining the spiritual, physical and emotional and integrating these, in so far as anyone can, to make a whole person.** While we all need to integrate these first three successfully, it is a mistake to rate finance with the same importance.

This is exactly where Frankl and logotherapy differ from the famous hierarchy of needs according to Maslow. Maslow believed that 'lower' needs as food, warmth, safety and security needed such to be satisfied to provide a foundation for higher needs leading finally to self-actualisation. This self-actualisation concept is that we become all that we are capable of being, fulfilling our complete potential. Very good work — if only life were that sweet for all.

One of my clients devoted her declining years, she was over 70 when we met, to caring for and trying to create a future for a son who had to struggle with bipolar mood swings and severe depression. He could, and did, smash walls in the house. His siblings advised her to have him put into care. But he was her son!

She had spent her adult life as a single mother, working as a cleaner and looking after four children. Now despite having no means of support beyond a pension she chose to stay with her son. Indeed last time we spoke she was determined to create a cleaning business and have her son handle the accounts. He could do that she believed.

Did this woman self-actualise? Did she achieve "everything" she was capable of being? She certainly transcended the self for the sake of others.

Frankl and Maslow debated this very issue in writing to each other. **Frankl believed that self-transcendence was a necessary condition if we are to achieve self-actualisation.** He further believed that self-transcendence flowed from, was a result of, meaning fulfilment. My client's meaning

was to look after her son. In doing that, I believe she indeed self-actualised in a much more important way than just achieving material success.

Don't hear me wrongly. I don't dispute the significance of finance — we all need to be aware of that both for oneself and others.

However, even if all is lost — when basics such as security, safety and even food and shelter are gone — the human being is still capable of taking a stand: a personal attitude to life that lifts the human being above the mere physical and psychological.

Let me explain further...

As a logotherapist I believe that the human person is three-dimensional. I sometimes use the Greek terminology which flows over into Psychology and Medicine.

First there is the body (*soma* – we are aware of somatic disorders); next the mind (psyche-we also affirm psychological disorders); and finally the spirit (*noos*). Frankl suggests that disorders of the spirit, noetic disorders, are simply an inability to cope with what life brings at this moment. They can express themselves in severe depression, anxiety, anger and the like, but essentially they are an inability to cope with a challenge of life.

I once had a Greek client to whom I explained this model at the appropriate time in therapy. As I mentioned the spirit (*noos*), his eyes grew wider and you could see he fully understood.

'Ah, *noosi*, yes that's very deep', he said. 'That is your essence.'

Since that time, I have tended to refer to the spiritual as our 'core self' or our 'essence'. It is this dimension that can take a stand despite deprivation, despite complete loss of all we have and have known.

Of course the human being is in fact indivisible. The three dimensions make one person. The 'essence' is where meaningful living originates, it is where we search for meaning in our lives, regardless of the circumstances.

I was interested that you placed 'spiritual' first on your list. Despite this, some recent surveys in Australia rate spirituality as something to which many people give a very low priority.

A much higher priority is given to self-enhancement or self-fulfilment — Maslow's lower order needs. If only more people understood that it is only when we include the *noetic* (spiritual) level that we become fully human.

Fulfilling the lower order needs will never produce happiness. Will finance do it? No, the world has lots of unhappy rich people. Genius or natural talent or education perhaps? There are plenty of examples of talented failures and uneducated derelicts. Only engaging with life, educated persisting in the search for meaning can bring happiness, along with a rich tapestry of other emotions.

Logotherapy operates at this *noetic* level, because that is where we find our meaning and where we are able to respond to life's challenge.

You blame many of the world's ills on organised religion. Certainly there have been numerous times over centuries when organised religion has indeed been the cause of much abuse. However, this tends to happen when religion and its adherents regard themselves as providing an answer to life, rather than providing a framework that can help us on the journey; the journey to find meaning that continues always. The search will end only with death.

Death? Most therapies stay away from the topic. **Logotherapy believes death is so important, as it makes each day lived so important.** It also has a strong belief in ultimate meaning. After all, if life has meaning at all, then surely there is a bigger picture, an overall meaning as part of this vast cosmos.

However, logotherapy does not pretend that it can define what that ultimate meaning actually is. If it is there it will be too complex for us to properly understand. No, **you must take your personal journey alone, as you grapple with life's questions and find meaning in your own life.**

For some, a religious framework can assist this journey and indeed there are many, both now and in the past, who have found that it does. However, it is a personal journey and that is important.

I enjoyed your comment on anti-depressants. Indeed we have an over-prescription and an over-dependence on these in our country. There is ample survey evidence to show that the number of prescriptions is increasing. Recently I noted that Australia ranks second in the world on the daily dose levels for anti-depressant prescriptions. The number of prescriptions has tripled over the past 15 years, and this in the "lucky country". These are increasing because we continue to look at human problems as something that can be 'fixed' or at least relieved. In the physical and psychological dimensions this is true. We can fix broken bones, lessen pain and reduce symptoms of severe anxiety with medication.

However, problems of the human spirit, caused by a lack of meaning in life or choosing pathways that were not meaningful, cannot be cured by medication. As I tried to make clear earlier noetic disorders are not able to be cured by medication, only the symptoms are cured that way.

When we have a difficult circumstance, as we will all experience, we start to look for simple answers that provide a 'quick fix'. Unfortunately, life is not like that and we

know this deep in our hearts. There is no such thing as stability in this spiritual (*noetic*) dimension.

We must understand that there will always be a tension in simply living life itself. It is a healthy tension and cannot be avoided. Indeed **life demands a healthy level of tension.** This type of tension occurs in the spiritual dimension (the *noos*), because that is where we grapple with meaning.

Constantly I have to try to explain to clients that no-one has a full pie. There will always be a piece missing. Sometimes we choose the piece we want to have missing; most times life itself simply creates that gap for us. It is all part of the tension of life.

Your reflections on finance are wise and undoubtedly realistic. It is prudent to meet Maslow's lower level needs, and good financial management might do this. The important realisation that we must have is that being financially secure or successful may be transient.

Despite our planning, it can all be gone in an instant. As Frankl and the other concentration camp prisoners realised when they were taken into custody, they had nothing left in life: "all we had left literally, was our naked existence."[6]

We came into this life naked and will exit it in a similar fashion. **Happiness is not something we can create: it follows on from what we achieve, our positive relationships and our attitude to life's unavoidable tensions.**

To put it succinctly, as a logotherapist, I believe that complete balance in the spiritual dimension is impossible to achieve, and it is indeed unhealthy if we think it can be achieved. In the physical and psychological dimensions, of course we should do whatever we can to ensure equilibrium and wellbeing.

Now to some advice on attitudes we can take to life:

Healthy Attitude:
I am a spiritual person. At all times, I can choose how I respond to the world around me.

Unhealthy Attitude:
My physical and emotional challenges are sometimes overwhelming. I can't cope.

Healthy Attitude:
A certain amount of tension in life is unavoidable.

Unhealthy Attitude:
At all costs, I must relieve stress in my life.

Healthy Attitude:
Happiness is a result of other parts of life being balanced or accepted.

Unhealthy Attitude:
If I am not happy, there must be something wrong.

RISK

You must have the courage to risk
and the expectation to win.

Mistakes are stepping stones to success. How can we ever grow, how can we ever learn, without taking risks? How can we ever get experience without making mistakes?

Life is a risky business. We never quite know, if we throw ourselves into life, what is going to happen next.

Even the word 'risk' is scary for some of us, but without it there is no reward!

Risk is about stepping into the unknown with trepidation but with the knowledge that, if we want to get the most out of life, we simply need to have risk-taking as one of our characteristics.

We do not need to replicate the explorers and sailors who discovered the world to maximise the adventure of life, but we do need to take some risks.

My trip with two friends overland, from India to London, was one that had been taken by numerous adventurers before us. We travelled from New Delhi to Pakistan through the notorious Khyber Pass (where every man carried a gun) into Kabul, across to Tehran, Turkey, Greece and then across Europe by bus and train. As in life, although millions have journeyed here before us, on this overland journey equally our experiences were, I am sure, very different to the experiences of others. These included being involved in an Indian movie with India's most famous movie star Dev Anand; being stranded in an Iranian city while our bus driver languished in jail; falling in and out of love; having just enough money to make it to London; and going on a safari in India, until we realised that the lions were actually in the car with us! So many more adventures and experiences! None of these experiences were planned and if had I been told in advance of all the risks of the journey I may never have gone.

At the Afghanistan/Iran border one of the passengers had to be left off the bus, as she did not have the right documents to get into Iran and there was nothing any one on the bus could do but hope she got safely back to Kabul. We had been told that thousands of young travellers disappeared at these borders every year and it was critical to have all the travel documents required. To that extent we planned to deal with the known risks. **Often in life we have to take unplanned risks.**

So just like the millions who have lived before us, each of our journeys will be different and discoverable only to us. Our journey of life is both external and internal: what and how we think is actually the key to opening the door of life. *90% of our lives are lived between our ears!*

Talking to strangers, although thoroughly discouraged to do so as a child, has been one of my favourite risks as a traveller and even when closer to home. We never know what might happen when we talk to strangers.

Recently I went to a small golf club near home to play a quick nine holes and try to improve my game. I noticed the person on the first tee before me was a very well-dressed, attractive man. I thought, 'Well, I can either wait behind him and play on my own, or ask if I could join him.'

He was happy to let me join him and so we started our round and our conversation. He was Italian and was in Melbourne to visit

his only son, married to an Australian. As the golf progressed, on my part rather badly, so did the conversation. He lived in Florence, one of my favourite cities in certainly one of my favourite countries.

As I drove him back to his son's house, we discussed the idea of a house swap. That sounded great to me — I could manage a five-minute walk to the Ponte Vecchio! A few months went by and emails started flying, regarding the idea of the house swap. It turned out that this charming man not only had an apartment in Florence but also in Milan and Bordighera, near Monte Carlo.

Suffice to say the house swap was a great success and we are still friends and I'm sure we will house swap again.

Yes, it was a risk to confront a stranger on the golf course. But my instincts told me that this man looked safe and the environment for the encounter (a golf course) is generally a place to meet like-minded people.

So while we can take advice from our parents and other mentors, **the spice of life is to try new things and put our toes in the water of risk.**

However, we need to know the boundaries of risk and to be wary of potential dangers.

After the hazardous but ultimately successful journey overland, I decided to go hitchhiking through Europe with a friend. We literally stood by the side of the road, thumbs up and waited for strangers to stop. At one stage in Austria we were given a lift by a young man who drove us into the nearest city, Graz, bought us dinner and was thoroughly charming. He then suggested we could stay at his family cottage up in the hills (of course, as hitchhikers, we never booked accommodation in. advance). The arrangement was that he would drive us up there, return to Graz and pick us up next morning.

Risk is about stepping into the unknown with trepidation but with the knowledge that, if we want to get the most out of life, we simply need to have risk-taking as one of our characteristics.

He had been charming, so we agreed. We found ourselves in a very pretty but totally remote cottage with an open fire, big doonas and perfect silence.

Our friend left us and promised to pick us up next morning at 9am. We got up in good time and waited for our new friend to arrive. We looked around our location; remote and alone was the best description. We actually had no idea where we were except that we had travelled back up the same highway we had hitchhiked into Graz and then turned off into the hills.

As the agreed time came and went, I started feeling nervous. I realised how far we were from Graz and any sign of habitation. I started to think that maybe we would be perfect game for our new friend and his friends. As I thought in colourful terms about rape and murder and started narrating the possible scenario to my friend, she thought I was being ridiculous. But I grew increasingly edgy and suggested to my friend that we start walking down this remote road. If we heard a car, we would hide until we were sure our new friend was on his own.

Time went by, three hours actually, and we were exhausted. By that time, both of us were extremely nervous and jumped behind bushes in advance of the two cars we heard coming towards us —neither contained our friend!

Finally, we arrived at the intersection of the main highway and we crossed over to head south back towards Graz. As was often the case, the first car that came by stopped and offered us a lift.

As we were getting in this car, another car came towards us and slowed down to turn up the road we had just walked for three hours. It was our friend, and the car was packed with his friends. There was no space for the two of us. My instincts had been right. We both felt sick at the idea of what could have happened to us and how long it would have taken for our bodies to be discovered, if ever.

To this day I have no idea why I felt the way I did. I had travelled through seemingly much more dangerous countries, but it seems to me that opportunity and danger can be very close. We need to be alert to both.

Risk, of course, can be much closer to home.

Some years ago, I decided to have a face lift. I had thought about this for some time and had seen some amazing results and some quite bad results. My research into cosmetic surgery had indicated that it was best to have it earlier, rather than later. I discussed that idea with some friends who were very much against the idea and told me extremely negative stories about women who had had cosmetic surgery. Not to be deterred, I met with two plastic surgeons and discussed the pros and cons. Of course, there is risk in all surgery and, with elective surgery, the risk feels greater because the surgery is not essential to life.

Having analysed the situation, I decided to go ahead! As my friends had been so negative, I did not let them know my decision, nor did I tell my family as I was sure they would not have supported the idea. I felt nervous enough taking this step without being fed any further negatives.

I went into the hospital feeling incredibly fearful. My only reassurance was that I had one of the best surgeons in the world!

When I woke up from the surgery, I could

not see. For just one second, I thought the surgery had blinded me! It was a terrifying moment, as I had totally placed myself in this position. It was like I had some sort of payback for being so vain! I have never felt so relieved in my life when a nurse held my hand and said, "you have bandages over your eyes; don't worry, everything is fine!"

Risk is something we have to decide for ourselves, after taking the best advice, weighing up the odds and then relying on our best judgement. We may find that in some parts of life we are significant risk-takers, while in others we are more cautious. But to be our best and to test our skills, we certainly need to get outside that comfort zone that can hold us back and hold us down.

Risk-taking becomes harder in a society where risk-avoidance is a key focus. My belief is that the nanny state mentality in many countries undermines human resolve and short sells what the human spirit is capable of. Risk-taking gives us a sense of self-belief and self-reliance.

I often see in Australia the difference in attitude between second and first generation migrants. The first generation risked all to come to this far-flung part of the world and so often succeeded .The second generation often lack the initiative, drive and risk-taking attitude of their parents.

There are, of course, risks not worth taking and some risks taken by others may seem purposeless to us. However, as each of us has a unique existence and unique way of thinking, one person's risk is another's challenge.

Almost anything I have done in life that has given me satisfaction has required risk. Not every risk taken has been positively rewarding but each has been energising and, at the very least, a learning experience.

The key with risk is to consider the possible outcomes and therefore minimise negative results. However, as with mountaineers, we never quite know when some external factor will come at us and change everything.

When my co-founder of griffin+row and I launched our product range, we had no idea that that our launch month would coincide with the month of the global financial crisis, which changed retail spending and business almost instantly. All we could do was look again at the situation and change direction. Yes, the outcome was not advantageous to our business, but we simply had to adapt and move on.

Tips for Risk:

✓ List the possible positive and negative outcomes from what you are contemplating.

✓ Expand that list to the best and worst outcomes.

✓ When you can, get advice from someone who has successfully done what you are planning.

✓ Avoid asking negative people for advice about what you are planning.

✓ Tune into your instincts

✓ Work out what your 'risk meter' tolerance is and stretch it a bit!

Taking risks and accepting fate

Marcia,

This section shows some wonderful insight, but I fear it also avoids one of life's major issues. Certainly we must take risks because no matter what we do, whether we like it or not, life itself is a risk. We do not really know the outcome of tomorrow, let alone next year!

Can we avoid risk? Can we simply do nothing? Even to take no decision is a risk in itself. So some form of risk is unavoidable and it's better to be as in control of it as if we can. So in Australian jargon, "have a go".

That is where fate comes in. You see, Marcia, encouraging the reader to take calculated risks is a good thing. What is left unsaid is that, when we do take that calculated gamble, we can feel we are in control of life. After all, if it does not turn out to be a 'win' then we accept the 'loss' and move on. If we have taken the risk wisely, then that loss will be acceptable. So we can go back to where we were. So called "calculated risks" assume an acceptable outcome, positive or negative.

But then we are sometimes confronted by results that we could never ever have contemplated. **The biggest risks in life are those things over which we have no control; we call this fate.** Where each of us is today, as you read this book, is a result of two things. First there are decisions ('risks' if you like) taken and then there is fate — what life simply throws at us.

One of my clients is afflicted with cerebral palsy. This is a condition that results from complications at birth so, from her perspective, it is uncontrollable; it was fate. Fortunately, she has physical rather than mental disabilities. Still, she must spend life in a wheelchair while being mentally alert. I cannot imagine how I would respond to being in that type of prison. But this is life for her. This is fate. Her task in life is to accept what life has brought and then to take an attitude to life that provides a meaningful existence and achieves that self-transcendence I mentioned earlier.

We are all confronted by fate but may not realise it. For instance, we did not choose our parents, where we were born or how

comfortable our childhood was. These are twists of fate or, if your framework for meaning includes this, a 'divine plan'. Either way, all we can do is to respond.

What will be the outcome of refusing to respond to life by doing nothing at all? Remember, doing nothing is a decision. Life will go on and there will be a result which will confront us with further challenges. So, if you choose to do nothing, choose that very carefully.

I am reminded in this of Frankl's own life story in the concentration camps. He survived by chance, while many died in the same situation.

Towards the end of Frankl's time in the camps, he was offered an opportunity to go to a 'rest camp' to look after patients. (By that time he had been recognised as a doctor and was looking after typhus patients, most of whom were terminal.)

Unfortunately, a 'rest camp' was often a euphemism for a trip to the gas chambers. While his friends urged him not to do so,

he eventually made the decision to go with people he knew and to continue look after his patients.

By happy accident, this 'rest camp' was true to name. Those who went were at least fed, while those who chose not to go and remained behind struggled to save themselves, given the lack of food. Some even resorted to cannibalism.

Frankl reflects in his book *Man's Search for Meaning* on the story Death in Tehran.

A rich and mighty Persian once walked in his garden with one of his servants. The servant cried that he had just encountered Death, who had threatened him. He begged his master to give him his fastest horse so that he could make haste and flee to Tehran, which he could reach that same evening. The master consented and the servant galloped off on the horse. On returning to his house the master himself met Death, and questioned him, 'Why did you terrify and threaten my servant?' 'I did not threaten him; I only showed surprise in still finding him here when I planned to meet him tonight in Tehran' said Death.

Your two opposite stories of good and possibly more difficult outcomes bring this into sharp focus. Fortunately, both had a happy ending. But as you point out, at least one, and perhaps either one, may not have done so. There is never a guarantee that any one story will have a happy ending.

So I agree that it is always important to look at what might happen and consider the options. It is important to list the possible outcomes and be aware of both the positives and negatives that may ensue.

However, life will always provide its own surprises and challenges. The challenge for each of us is always that, having done our best, having made the plans and put in the effort, we must then take responsibility for whatever the outcome may be.

We also need to realise that there is always a chance that the outcome may be at least somewhat beyond our control.

The challenge is to respond to the next question life asks of us, realising that it is I who is asked. It is I who will be asked to respond, whether as a result of taking a risk or of deciding to hide and take no risk whatsoever.

Healthy Attitude:
Life is a risk—blows of fate can come at any time.

Unhealthy Attitude:
Avoid all risk—it is best to stay safe.

Healthy Attitude:
Where I am today is a result of my decisions: some good, some bad, and fate. All I can do now is to start from where I am.

Unhealthy Attitude:
I got where I am today, successful or not, entirely through my own efforts.

Healthy Attitude:
I am at least partially responsible for where I am today; and fully responsible now for what I choose to do with that.

Unhealthy Attitude:
I am not responsible for where I am today; I really had no say in it.

We also need to realise that there is always a chance that the outcome may be at least somewhat beyond our control.

SELF-BELIEF

The person who cannot believe
in himself cannot
believe in anything else.

If we don't both believe in **and** value ourselves, who else will? This does not mean we need to be full or ourselves or overconfident about our skills, but rather we need to accept and appreciate what talents we do have, what values we hold and how we can best utilise them.

In this world dominated by celebrities, it is easy to put ourselves down. Why aren't we as clever, as rich, as thin and as beautiful as those we constantly see in the media? Actually, a lot of what we see has been so photoshopped that these fabulous faces and bodies are greatly elevated from their original state!

There will always be someone thinner, richer, more beautiful, cleverer and on the list goes. We simply have to be the best we can be and honour what we have been endowed with.

Of course we all have flaws, but we need to work on these and accept that we are not perfect. No-one is.

As Leonard Cohen says so beautifully: "There is a crack in everything; that is how the light gets in".

Self-belief comes from a really deep place and, with positive parenting, can start in early childhood.

I feel so grateful that my father, who loved sport, was such a great encourager and supporter of my sporting prowess as a child. I think the small successes I had as a young sports-girl gave me very healthy self-belief.

Our self-belief is tested on a daily basis, mine has been tested time and again. The way I have been able to work on self-belief is to put myself out there for challenges in business, in sporting activities and in doing things that I feel initially nervous about undertaking. I have also been careful about whose opinions I take notice of.

I remember a very close, very wealthy and beautiful friend of mine who once commented that, although she had all these attributes, she did not have the level of self-belief that I seemed to have.

The life my friend lived was very peer-related. She was extremely dependent on her partners and had not adventured much in life, outside her highly competitive and wealthy circle. She never felt worthy, despite her physical beauty and her generous nature. She demonstrated very clearly to me that self-worth is not directly related to net worth.

Belief in oneself comes from going outside

For a short time in my life as a young married, I did feel the power of the peer group. But as my marriage collapsed, money disappeared and the good life gone for a time, I was left to my own devices to rebuild.

I was fortunate to meet a business mentor who encouraged me to go out and restart my life with confidence. I owe a huge debt of gratitude to this man, as he constantly reminded me what I could do, which countered my negative thoughts and lack of confidence.

Self-belief does not just appear in our lives; it is developed through what we do, how we challenge ourselves and what risks we take to achieve what we want.

Sometimes we even have to fake it to make it!

I remember my first serious business presentation to around two hundred women at a major Melbourne hotel. I rehearsed and rewrote it for days and did not sleep the night before. My self-doubt was overwhelming: who was I to talk about skincare when I had just started the business? These were all successful women — why would they believe what I had to say about these products?

I was literally worried sick about this presentation but, of course, had to appear confident and knowledgeable. As the audience started to arrive, I really had to put on a very brave face and as I stood to speak I could actually hear my knees knocking. This was an extreme challenge for me.

At the end there was applause and I was greeted with comments like: *You are such a polished speaker.* I was amazed and delighted that no-one had any idea that I was literally terrified about giving the presentation. The lesson was clear: if I was to become a confident public speaker (which was an essential requirement for my role in building that business), I would need to take myself out of my

comfort zones, being prepared to stand on your own two feet and doing your best, challenging yourself, celebrating successes and learning from mistakes.

I started my education in the local primary school and moved on to boarding schools. I never felt part of the 'in crowd'. (And girls/women can be so mean to each other!) I somehow never managed to be 'cool', so it was interesting to attend my school reunion recently and to hear one of the 'coolest' girls who belonged to the 'coolest' group explain that, because she was so dominated by this group at school, she was totally lost when she left school and had done nothing since in terms of a career. I was astounded, as I had always seen her as intelligent and beautiful. Even more enviable was her perfect French accent, with RRRRs that rolled in a way I could never emulate!

comfort zone until public speaking became second nature to me.

Now I jump at the chance to speak to audiences of any size and have great confidence. However even now, after thousands of presentations, I still feel nerves rising as I stand to speak as each new audience is a new opportunity to succeed or fail. The good news is that my knees no longer knock together with fear!

On an emotional level, I have found it equally important to work on self–belief.

As a woman, and for a long period in my life, a single woman, it has taken a lot of 'self-talk' to be prepared to be alone if I need to be, and not allow myself to cave into relationships that do nothing for my self-esteem. I distinctly remember an incident that I later reflected on as one that made me feel good about myself.

I had been to a dinner party and met up with an attractive man I had known for a long time but had never had any romantic interest in and it seemed to be vice versa. He offered to escort me to my home after dinner and, when we arrived, asked himself in for coffee. We know that this is generally a euphemism for something more!

I looked at him and said "Sorry, I won't ask you in; I need to be adored by a man and I know you don't feel that way." He looked a bit surprised but simply said okay and that was that!

What we say to ourselves, and equally to each other, is so important. We can play a valuable role by standing up for ourselves and supporting and encouraging those worthy of our support. It can be in the simplest ways, smiling at strangers and complimenting people on their achievements. The way people respond to deserved compliments is a good reminder that there is not enough of this!

Each day as we go through life, **we need to think about who we have elevated and encouraged.** These people may be complete strangers!

Some years ago, I read about a young student who had received an award from his community for taking care of his young

brother. The mother of these boys had died of cancer and the father had abandoned them many years before. The older brother had to postpone his studies to look after his sibling.

I was very touched by this story. I wondered whether, with all these tragedies, he would he grow up to have belief in the world and belief in himself. I rang the journalist to see if there was anything I could do to help this young man. The journalist called me back after a few days and said the older brother would be pleased to meet me. So I made contact and drove to the town where he lived outside Melbourne. He was a delightful young man and it seemed that he needed to get a part-time job to finance his studies and to be close to his brother. I knew of a large accounting firm in the western suburbs of Melbourne and wondered if they might be able to assist. I told my contact there the story and he agreed to meet this young man. The outcome was that he was given a part-time job which enabled him to continue his studies and care for his brother.

I have no idea where that young man is now but I got deep satisfaction from this small effort. I did this because the story really touched my heart and I wanted in some way to ensure this young man could resume his studies, secure his future and, in turn, enhance his self-belief.

Recently, I sent an email to a politician, who was part of the panel on a very difficult enquiry into child abuse. I congratulated her for having the courage, along with the other members of the panel, to seek the truth, to question very strongly those giving evidence despite their elevated titles, and to expose and condemn those institutions that have abused the trust of thousands of children and, by so doing destroyed their lives.

The stories of these victims always speak about how their self-belief and self-worth were damaged by the monsters who abused them.

The politician was so pleased to receive my short email. She said it meant a lot to her that people felt that her work was worthwhile. We need to encourage and congratulate people, no matter what their status in society. Everyone benefits from encouragement and support at all levels in the community.

I wonder if, as a society, we do give enough praise to worthy people who do amazing things for the betterment of the community. Or do we just go along with the group and media adulation of often unworthy footballers, celebrities and anyone else whose behaviour consumes the media?

As Australians we are famously better at knocking than encouraging. **But a small word of encouragement, or a kind and genuine compliment, can go a long way.**

Self-worth is a quality that everyone needs to have. We can only benefit as a community from individuals who strive to be their best and, in so doing, learn to believe in themselves.

Tips for Self-belief:

✓ Be kind in your self–evaluation.

✓ Be kind to yourself!

✓ Be firm about where you can do better.

✓ Encourage and compliment others—but be genuine when doing so.

✓ Make a daily habit of helping someone feel better about themselves, even a stranger in the street!

The meaning of self-belief

Marcia,

I agree that belief in one's self can be evidenced by going outside comfort zones and being prepared to take a stand. However, if the motivation is only towards my own achievement and my own satisfaction, I will eventually find it hollow.

Human beings know this deep down, but can be distracted from finding meaning in so many ways. In his book *Conversion*, Malcolm Muggeridge quotes an inscription written centuries ago in the Libyan desert: "I, a captain of a legion of Rome, have come to know this truth, there are but two things in life to be sought, love and power. And no man has both."

To me, the writer has discovered the truth that, as Einstein says, "Only a life lived for others is worthwhile". I must focus outwards, towards others. That is why I find your tips excellent; they challenge you to be better by also encouraging others on their journey. **Remember that the greatest human desire is to find meaning in life.** It is unique to each person and each situation, but it is there. But how to find it?

There are three ways in which we can find meaning in our lives. The first is in what we create or build as part of our life. For many of us, this is our work. It is also family, home or whatever we develop that is a gift to this world. Yes, that takes self-belief at times, and sometimes just sheer determination. Not every workplace is interesting or joyful and no real family is like the Brady Bunch. We can choose to make these situations meaningful by the way we decide to approach others, and by the attitude we take ourselves.

One of my recent clients had taken a new job just to support the family after his own business, with a multi-million dollar turnover, went to the wall. Working for someone else and doing what he was scheduled to do was not easy after so many years of being in charge. At our first session he told me how his new boss had said recently "you act as though you really don't want to be here." We explored how employees acted when they seemed as though they appreciated their work. After all, he admitted that he needed this job for the sake of the family.

Finally, we decided that for the coming week he would "Act as if…" he liked the work. It made all the difference. By next week he was telling me that he felt better about life and was more productive at work. It is not

always easy to find meaning in our work, but by changing the way he responded he had found new meaning in what he was doing.

The second way to find meaning in life lies in our capacity to experience the wonderful world in which we live and those who share it with us. The capacity to experience nature, music, the wonder of the stars at night and perhaps even to marvel at life itself are all experiences of meaning. It can be more meaningful to be swept up in a wonderful piece of music or the magnificence of a sunset than to be stuck only with the material issues of life and the challenges that surround us daily.

By far the deepest experience of meaning will be in relating deeply with another person and responding to them. That is learning to relate in all three dimensions of our being — body, mind and spirit — and particularly spirit. *I can only become me in relating to you.* That is a great motto for life.

The third way to find meaning in life, and this is the most important thing to realise, is through the attitude we take when we are challenged by unavoidable situations. I told you about my recent client. Yes, he found meaning in his work, and did so by taking an attitude to what was unavoidable. I emphasise *attitude* and *unavoidable* here. We will all have to face them; the loss of a loved one and our own death to name but two. But most of our meaning will be found in what we create and how we experience our world, hence the strength of your excellent tips in this chapter.

Now I want to change focus for just a short time here. **I suggest that real self-belief centres on knowing who you are in the first place.**

Unfortunately, we often describe ourselves in terms of things we have or things we have achieved.

Sometimes in therapy, I will do an exercise with a client that asks them to write down five sentences about themselves. I invite you (and

I am . . .

1. _____

   _____

2. _____

   _____

3. _____

   _____

4. _____

   _____

5. _____

   _____

the reader) to try this exercise. Try it right now please – five sentences to describe who you are.

What did you write? Did you begin by saying that you are a business woman, an engineer, a mother of two or whatever? If you remain at that level, you will very soon run out of sentences and probably you won't get to five. If you do get to five in this manner, it is likely to provide only a shallow description.

Did you eventually come to write sentences like, 'I am unsure of myself' or 'I am seeking friendships?' One of my clients kept on about job, career and family until we got to number four, when, after a long pause, she said "actually, I'm a very lonely person." Now we could work with that and we did so.

You see, if you know who you are at depth, this goes beyond whether or not you are a successful young sportswoman, an entrepreneur or whatever. If you know the real 'you', this in turn can lead to a very healthy self-belief. So the other achievements, important and inspiring as they are, matter little. As I have said already:

> "It matters not the radius of your circle but how well you fill its scope." (Frankl)

You see it matters little what has happened in the past. Of course, it can affect where you are now; indeed it has brought you here. We talked about that before when we spoke about "fate" and "risk". However, how you respond NOW, from where you are, however you got here, is a decision you take and an attitude you take to life. That is your self-belief, but at a much deeper level. **You now realise you are unique in this universe and must respond to the questions life asks each of us.**

Of course, your decision or decisions will be limited by the options that you may have.

In some ways life is like a game of chess and Frankl compares life to a chess game in his book, *The Doctor and the Soul*.

When confronted by adversity, we have a tendency, like a child, to sweep the chess pieces

If you know the real 'you', this in turn can lead to a very healthy self-belief.

off the board. On the other hand, perhaps we also decide to try to move a piece or two while the opponent is not watching!

Real self-belief will have us decide to continue to play the game and play it to its very end, whether we win or lose. That is what life expects from us. We are asked, and we must answer.

How should we live our life? What is the best move? We need to believe that we can take a meaningful decision, in spite of all adversity, and that this will in turn create a better direction.

I agree with you we must strive to do our best and learn to believe in ourselves. However, this leads us to constantly question each day, 'What is the best thing to do?'

In life as in chess, there is no one 'best move'. It depends on where the pieces are on the board.

The individual who makes meaning-filled responses and decisions in the face of life's challenges, who aspires to be the best human being they can be, generates both real achievement and a settled conscience. **This is real self-belief: "I can rise above whatever circumstance comes my way".**

Healthy Attitude:
Purpose is what you do, meaning is who you are—life can always have meaning.

Unhealthy Attitude:
I can't seem to find any purpose in my life.

Healthy Attitude:
You can always choose your attitude, even if there are no other possible choices.

Unhealthy Attitude:
Sometimes life leaves me with no options.

Healthy Attitude:
How I respond to life defines who I am.

Unhealthy Attitude:
My status and what I achieve make me who I am.

PERSPECTIVE

The only thing that is subjective
is the perspective through
which we approach reality.

— *Viktor Frankl*

Just when things seem really tough in life, a wonderful attribute called perspective can give us just that. Perspective is like a telescope to help us see, from a greater distance, our perceived and actual problems.

For years now, I have used these thoughts as my perspective when all seems to be going wrong:

There are more than 7 billion people on the planet, possibly half have to worry about putting food on the table every day, another 2 billion have to worry about a roof over their heads, of the last 1.5 billion, maybe 1 billion are doing jobs simply to take care of the above! That leaves around half a billion people on this planet who live lives where they have real choices over and above food and shelter, and may even be working at something they enjoy!

I can't vouch for these figures, but I have a sense that they could be in the ballpark.

Living in a western democracy, while things may not be perfect (or even far from perfect depending on one's view of the world) we are the lucky ones. **The problems we have that sometimes seem insurmountable become miniscule, if we take a bigger perspective.** I call them first world problems, as opposed to third world problems!

When we read about wars, destructive floods, typhoons, fires and the plight of women in some Islamic societies and increasingly the consequences of Islamic extremism, the issues in our lives take on a lesser significance.

I remember being quite shocked when I heard a woman complaining that her cleaner had broken her hand. At first, I thought her complaint stemmed from the fact that the cleaner would now be unable to work and therefore not be paid. But to my dismay, her complaint stemmed from the fact that she now had the inconvenience of having to find a new cleaner or, heaven forbid, do the cleaning herself for a few weeks!

Recently, I had an interesting experience meeting a young woman from Mongolia and tuning into her life and its challenges.

I was walking out of the city in Melbourne and was about to cross a park in the dark, then thought better of it. As I started changing direction, I noticed a young woman of Asian appearance about to do what I had planned. I approached her and suggested that she walk with me, as I felt that walking alone in that park was dangerous.

As we crossed the path together, she told me her story. She was from Ulan Bataar, the capital of Mongolia, and was alone in Melbourne completing a course in International Studies at Melbourne University. She was looking for accommodation in the area she was walking to. Once we had crossed the park together, I drove her to the address where

she was looking for accommodation. We stopped outside a rather gloomy, dilapidated block of flats in a dark part of the street. I gave her my telephone number in case she needed some help, and also took her mobile phone number.

As I drove away, I thought about her life. She had left her two children with her mother to do her university course and improve her employment prospects. She was 30 and her husband had left her for a younger woman. (Now that is a different perspective — apparently it is a way of life in Mongolia to be an old woman at thirty and rejected by one's husband!)

I thought about how lonely she must be, as she had no friends in Melbourne and had spent her first three months studying English to prepare herself for the university course.

Perspective is like a telescope to help us see, from a greater distance, our perceived and actual problems.

I drove to the country that weekend, taking the same road that my parents had taken when they dropped me off at boarding school a long way from home. I remembered the loneliness of that separation — same state, same country, but nothing compared to the journey and distance between Melbourne and Ulan Bataar, Mongolia!

I could not stop thinking about this young woman and her story and decided to call her on return to Melbourne. I called the number she had given me many times but to no avail. Finally she called me back, she had had phone problems and had not received my calls.

She told me that she had found accommodation in a much less desirable part of the city and I invited her to my house to see a room I could offer her. She explained that she had paid rent in advance but when she arrived at my house she simply said "Yes, I want to stay here." She arranged to sublet her apartment and she stayed with me for three months.

She told me a lot about her life in Mongolia and it truly put mine into perspective. She felt that she had had to leave her family and country to improve her employment options and her family's lifestyle. She was amazed at the amenities in my home, no mansion but the usual Australian lifestyle gadgets. **There is nothing like sharing one's home with someone from a completely different culture to put one's life in perspective!**

As a young student and later, I had travelled the world from Calcutta to London overland and all over Asia and Europe. These travels were generally during university holidays, while my fellow students were often at the family beach house. These trips were

exhilarating and always challenging; the value of student travel is that you get to see the world from a different perspective, the hospitality of impoverished villagers sharing their meagre meal, the simple happiness of people with no material goods and the kindness of strangers.

When I returned from these travels, I was always astounded at the narrow lives many of my friends and university peers were living. Of course, it does not take long to fall into that mode and become equally concerned about things of little real consequence!

As my life changed from being the young wife of a glamorous high income lawyer, I always had the images of my travels in my mind. So when my life fell apart, I had a different perspective to fall back on. I was aware that, while my life had taken a difficult turn, I was far ahead of so many millions of people.

Each time I see a blind person or someone with some other disability, it's impossible not to feel lucky and put minor problems in perspective. **The value of having perspective is powerful and can assist us in getting on with life.**

Tips for Perspective:

✓ Estimate where you are on the ladder of good fortune in the human race!

✓ Ask yourself whether the issue will matter in one year's time.

✓ Find a few things to be happy about every day.

✓ Ask for help from someone who is wise and kind.

The 'Collective Neurosis': evidence of an ailing society

Marcia,

I spend a lot of my hours with clients helping them to see life events through a different lens. One of my clients had returned to Australia from overseas work to be closer to his children and reconnect with them. Unfortunately, when he came back here he was reduced to living off his accumulated savings. He could not find a job.

During one particular session he was particularly depressed and down. The conversation went like this, with some further comments recorded on the whiteboard in our room:

Client: "Life has not been fair."

Paul: "Why should it be?"

Comment: You have always risen to life's challenges – life is not fair – it just asks questions.

Client: "No one appreciates my ability."

Paul: "No one? Do they need to? Or is your own understanding enough?"

Comment: Your class likes your work (he had taken on, very successfully, volunteer tutoring for English with students whose native language was not English). You are using different skills now.

Client: "I have given up so much, home, kids, and I'm left with nothing."

Paul: "Did you do it for them or for you?"

Comment: You did it for them – so it's a gift.

Client: "My parents never saw me play sport, or music…"

Comment: So you are determined to give this to your own kids!

As a logotherapist I try to do more than simply apply a set of techniques to 'cure' someone. **First of all, logotherapy is a philosophy of life and you have to live that way yourself.** Then, for the therapist, the techniques are there simply to help others see that key message for themselves: *My life has meaning!*

We need to realise we are not here today, in this world, at this place, only because we chose to be. We had some part in it of course, but **the path we have trodden to be here at this time and in this particular society was not fully chosen by us.** And hence we each have a responsibility to respond to the life we have, since it is the only one we do have.

Frankl has said that, rather than study abnormal cases, it could perhaps be better at times for psychologists and therapists to look at the ordinary person in the street. **They have placed life in perspective and intuitively know how to cope and recover from life's adversities.** Discovery of meaning in life, for many ordinary people, is intuitive.

Unfortunately, as I look at our society, I see that these days we tend to respond instead by succumbing to what Frankl calls the 'collective neurosis'. Neurosis is an older term for what mental health practitioners call today a 'disorder'. **Frankl believed that a whole society can be 'disordered'.** (I have used the term 'neurosis', so that those who read further and engage with Frankl's original work have a

consistent terminology). He had experienced a debilitating societal disease himself, one that created the concentration camps and the holocaust. The holocaust was an attempt by one political caste to exterminate a whole race of people because of their religious beliefs. Few stood against it; most preferring to remain silent, anonymous and, hence, safe.

What would we have done in this circumstance? Turned a blind eye or stood up? We don't know. We hope we never have to face such a stark challenge. However, each time we have a perspective that is focused only on ourselves and forget to focus outwards, towards the welfare of others, we recreate in our own small way this collective disease.

This collective disorder in society is characterised by beliefs such as:

＊ I have no possibility of changing my life or having an influence upon it

＊ live for today, just enjoy yourself

＊ don't stand out in the crowd

＊ hold on to what you have lest others take it (or even ask to share it)

Ultimately, the lack of meaning here will weigh us down. **We can make a difference – we must believe that if we are to believe in a meaning for our life.** We are unique, and that is profound. If we really believe that each person is unique then what we do is not only important, its contribution will never be repeated. Each person affects the lives of others, just by what we do and who we are each day.

It was Robert Kennedy, in his funeral oration for JFK, who suggested that each time we stand up against tyranny we send out a tiny ripple of hope that can become an irresistible wave. I suggest that each time we turn a blind eye to injustice and the needs of others we crush that hope.

Your story of the woman complaining about her cleaner provides an example of this. Rather than be concerned about the person and her welfare, she remains totally immersed in the self. She does not realise she is affecting lives around her, nor does she seem to care.

This is an attitude that says 'live for myself alone and for today only and take no notice of those around me.'

We have another example of this in the myopic fear we tend to have in our own country of immigrants and refugees. 'Others' from strange backgrounds are feared until we meet them as individuals and real people.

Finally, there are two points I want to make to you.

First, as Frankl says: "Life teaches most people that we are not here to enjoy ourselves". In fact, **most people experience more challenges and more unpleasurable sensations daily than they experience pleasurable sensations.** That is reality. If we are open to it, we learn much more about life and ourselves from the negative experiences than from the pleasant ones.

Secondly, we are much more than material beings. As far as we know, a herd of cows does not much care how beautiful the sunset is, nor can they possibly conceive that this earth is but a sphere in a vast cosmos.

Are we not rather taught by 'inner experience', by ordinary living unbiased by theories, that our natural pleasure in a beautiful sunset is 'in a way more real' than, say, astronomical calculations of the time when the earth will crash into the sun?

—*The Doctor and the Soul*, Frankl

This is a human experience. **Recognising the beauty of what we have and where we are puts life in perspective.** Realising that life will always challenge us, and that the particular human quality we have gives us the power to respond to any circumstance, is the perspective that we need to have and that Frankl's logotherapy invites us to welcome.

Healthy Attitude:

There will always be aspects of life I cannot control. What I can always control is how I choose to respond to what life brings.

Unhealthy Attitude:

Life is not fair—bad things seem to keep happening to me.

Healthy Attitude:

To find meaning I must look beyond myself; the greatest experiences in life are other people and life itself.

Unhealthy Attitude:

Life is short, so just look after number one. I'm here for a good time, not a long time!

Healthy Attitude:

No-one knows when it is going to be his or her hour to stand up and be counted.

Unhealthy Attitude:

Don't stand out in the crowd; stand back.

> Each person affects the lives of others, just by what we do and who we are each day.

VISION

A flower is a weed
seen through joyful eyes.

Vision implies a look at life beyond today's activities.

How will my life look in five or ten years? What do I need to do to change, if I really want to achieve that vision of the future?

We achieve our vision by setting short-term chunked down goals, step by step.

We need to do this because the gradient between where we are now and where we may want to go can simply be too high. Sometimes we just can't get started because of that perceived gradient.

During one year of my life, I had a clear geographical vision of where I wanted to be. England was the final destination of my trip. But as is the case so often in life, I did not know exactly how I would get there!

As my mother drove me to the airport in Melbourne, she said, "I notice your ticket says Melbourne, Hong Kong, Calcutta—that seems a long way from England."

However, behind this very vague start there was a plan of sorts. My two friends and I knew which countries we had to go through to get to England: India, Pakistan, Afghanistan, Iran, Turkey, Greece and then through the reminder of Europe. We just did not know exactly which transport we would take after Calcutta or how long it would take.

In many ways, as is the case in life, **it is sometimes best not to know the obstacles and difficulties ahead or we may not undertake the journey!** We had, for example, no intention of spending three months in India or three weeks working on a movie in Kathmandu with Dev Anand, one of India's most famous actors ever! We had actually gone to Kathmandu to go trekking; but when we recognised Dev Anand in a hotel lobby and heard he was directing and acting in a movie set in Kathmandu, we simply could not resist the opportunity to work with him.

That experience was a one-off. The movie *Hare Rama Hare Krishna* was quite controversial, as it was about the bad influence of western hippies over young Indians. Those three weeks are etched in my memory. Every time I think about persuading dozens of the hippies to appear in the discotheque scene, as well as actually painting the walls of the downstairs hotel bar to make it look like a discotheque, it makes me realise that we can actually do pretty much what we set out to do with enough determination!

We did not know that we'd have to travel through a town in the Khyber Pass, where every man carried a gun. (Of course, we know that now, after the way that history has panned out in that part of the world.) We did not know that our bus driver would end up in jail in Iran, for carrying a local hitchhiker who was killed as he tripped getting off the bus. We had no idea that the driver would be held liable for an act of kindness that went wrong; we did not know that the widow would have to be compensated and that our fellow travellers, and even the bus company, did not have sufficient resources to pay up!

Similarly, when I started my Pola business, I had a vision to rebuild my life financially by building a large and successful business. However I had little idea how I would do this initially, as I had come from the life of being a corporate economist.

But as with anything that is of value in life, success rarely happens overnight. Some people take a lifetime to achieve their vision, while for others the journey may not be quite so onerous.

Unlike my trip overland to England, my business journey was step by step over a sixteen-year time span. Not every step was upwards; there were numerous obstacles to overcome. There was no advertising budget

for this brand; I had no idea about how to sell; no-one had heard of the products; the packaging was very ordinary; and I knew very little about skincare and cosmetics when I started out. So the list of obstacles went on and on.

In many ways, the journey was not unlike the overland trip and, in a strange way, that trip prepared me for the hazards of my business journey. Every day was full of challenges and, as each one was faced and dealt with, another would appear. The great thing was that because I had overcome each problem along the way, when one reappeared I had developed the tools to deal with it.

The biggest obstacle was, of course, my own thoughts. Can I really do this? What if I fail? Who will believe in me? Where will I find the salespeople? The doubting went on and on.

I started to read motivational books, and attended seminars on selling. **Then I started to understand the importance of my own thinking: I could choose to be a positive problem solver or simply accept defeat!** As I grew in confidence about the products and my own ability to sell and recruit sales people, the vision started to become a reality. It took a long time — sixteen years in fact — but each year along the way saw some progress and that kept the vision real.

Honestly, had I foreseen and worried about all the possible obstacles on that journey I may not have achieved the vision I had of a successful business and resultant financial security.

So with life, it is helpful to have a vision for where we want to be, without letting that vision become so narrow that we miss out on adventures along the way!

Tips for Vision:

✓ Take time out to think about where you want to be in five years.

✓ Don't worry if you can't see the vision clearly; it will become clearer as you move in the direction you want to go.

✓ Don't expect to have the answer for tomorrow, today—much of that is in the journey.

✓ Understand that there will be mistakes, corrections, disappointments along the way.

Living life looking forward, rather than in the rear vision mirror

Marcia,

This is a good time in this book to remind our readers of the key points of logotherapy. Meaning-filled living certainly requires vision in three ways:

* A belief that life has meaning at all times, even in the most difficult circumstances.

* A conviction that there is an ultimate meaning in our life and our universe. However, whatever that ultimate meaning may be, it is well be beyond our full understanding.

* A realisation that we can CHOOSE to find the unique meaning in life that belongs to us.

Life either has meaning or it does not. If it does not, there is little point in prolonging it or seeking all of the wonderful experiences that you describe. It has meaning even at the very end, when perhaps we are powerless to do much more than grasp what little is left of it.

I am reminded of a wonderful client who told me that his aim when he was young was to reach the ripe old age of 84. Now he could see this coming – next birthday! He had reached this milestone in life and now struggled with the concept of death.

At this stage of his life my task was first to convince him that his legacy was something to treasure. Here was a man who had supported his wife and three kids through thick and thin. When his fencing business went bad

he had worked at height on major building projects, ten or twenty floors up, overcoming his innate fear of doing so. On another job he stood up and told a workforce of a hundred or more that their union-backed campaign against the company could only lead to it going broke and them losing their jobs. It was not a popular message but he was right. Courage in the face of fear, even though they did not listen.

We spent many hours on this, understanding his legacy. The legacy each of us leaves behind will outlast our existence. **"It matters not that we have to leave this world eventually"**, Frankl says, **"but that we have something to leave from".**

We all want to be remembered and this man had much to be remembered for. **Our next step was to look at developing a real meaning for this last journey, of unknown duration.** I asked him what life expected of him now, in these last days, but not directly.

"What do you want your children to say at your Eulogy?" I asked. Then I suggested some answers:

"Dad lived positively right to the end. Whenever we visited we always felt welcome and that he was interested only in us."

OR

"Dad lived a great life but towards the end he just seemed to despair. He shut himself away and did not want to see anyone."

We decided on the first. The only tool any person eventually has when facing the end of life, is our attitude. So our vision must always be focussed on what life expects, what we are challenged to do now, for as long as we are capable of a response. Life always as meaning, logotherapy lesson one.

On the other hand, as human beings our vision is limited. We "see" and experience the world only through a limited lens.

Surely we are above other life forms? Yes, in many ways, but sometimes we lack their skills. We do not have the navigation capacity of some insects and birds, or the capacity to hear some of the sounds our dog might hear. On the other hand, human beings have something beyond other life forms. **We have always had a yearning to 'make sense of it all', to find the meaning in our existence.** That is the second basic belief of the logotherapist; we all crave for meaning.

Finally, we logotherapists believe that each person can choose to find that meaning in life that is uniquely theirs. But where does this meaning fit within this vast cosmos? After all we know we inhabit only a miniscule part, spaceship earth?

We long to know if there is an ultimate meaning for life. Is this possible to know? No, we can only believe it to be so.

Life will remain a mystery. The great scientists realise this. They explain what happens—for instance that gravity is the attraction of two objects towards each other. They can even calculate how it happens. How fast will the cricket ball falls when dropped from the tower? But the 'why', the reason all of this happens and can be measured, the ultimate question, is shrouded in mystery.

To make sense of life, to 'understand' it, we can only have faith that there is meaning beyond what we can comprehend. Frankl says that 'we must be imbued with a profound belief in ultimate meaning.' He suggested that our struggle with the concept of an ultimate meaning comes from our limited vision. We see the world from where we are. The ordinary ant, or even your dog, surely cannot conceive of other continents and huge oceans. Human beings know these things, but it would be presumptuous to believe that we have a universal knowledge of reality within the cosmos.

pathways that have led us to where we are today hide many accidental intersections.

However, we must not use the past as an excuse. Looking backwards can lead us to succumb to the temptation of 'if only'. *If only I had chosen the other job. If only I had different parents. If only I had not married when I did. In other words, What would have happened if...?*

All of these are really non-questions. Had any of these and so many other life issues been different, you would not be the person you are now, today. The person you are now, today, is what you have to work with and this is the person questioned now, today, by life itself, not some fictional imaginary other.

Where we stand today is, of course, also the result of decisions we have taken. Good or bad, for better or for worse, they have made us who we are now, and there is no going back. I often have to help my clients to live life looking forwards, rather than continually looking in the rear vision mirror. Of course, if you drive that way you must crash!

A glance in the mirror is good occasionally. It is true that who we are today is the result of our past. So a difficult childhood, a lack of love and attachment in early years, can affect our capacity to relate and respond. Freud's genius, which Frankl respected absolutely, was to realise this.

The insight Frankl brought to therapy was that, while we are determined by our past, **we are not absolutely determined by the past.** What we do today, now, is our decision.

Yes, we have been shaped, sometimes scarred, by the past. However, we have the capacity always to respond NOW to what faces us today. So that is our vision, to look forward from here, to take a stand, to set a pathway. Yes, that is vision made real.

No, we must struggle with the concept of 'ultimate meaning' and believe that life has this in some way; else it has no meaning at all. The religions, of course, have developed frameworks that include ultimate meaning. But their descriptions of it are incomplete, as they must be, and perhaps for some they don't ring true because they use terms and concepts based on this limited vision of reality.

All we can do is to live now, today, with that basic trust that our life makes a difference.

In the here and now, life can often only be properly understood as we look backwards. This was the first step for my octogenarian client. The maze of tracks and crossing

Where you are today creates your destiny. It is part of a journey that has been shaped by your decisions, yet has also been created by fate.

Our long-term goal must be to experience this world and to carve out a life, to create something. Time is a friend and while we still have time we can take decisions and set directions, even if we legitimately can say our past is strewn with defeats and disasters.

In our most difficult times, it can seem that life has no meaning. Yet there is always something left, and we are challenged to find that. How often have we seen people who have lost homes in fires or floods but are able to say, *We still have our family?*

It is vital we have something or someone to live for. However, sometimes we have to diligently search for it and find it. No-one can do this for us – and it is always there.

As I have said earlier, meaning in life can be found in three ways:

* By what we create.

* By our very experience of life itself. And finally, if we have no other path to take...

* By the attitude we adopt to life.

In a meaning-centred approach to life, we will always have something that we want to create. This is often achieved in our day-to day-work but, at different stages of life, may be achieved through family, friends or some aspect of our career. **The experience of intimate friendships, of love, of selfless devotion to another and just of this amazing world in which we live is the second path to meaning.** Ultimately, when there is nothing else, we can choose our attitude.

Healthy Attitude:
Life always has meaning, and I can find it. But its ultimate meaning will remain a mystery.

Unhealthy Attitude:
Life is meaningless.

Healthy Attitude:
The fact that I live now, even if only in small ways, will make this world a better or worse place. That is my legacy.

Unhealthy Attitude:
When I'm gone, there will be nothing left.

Healthy Attitude:
There is always a choice, even if it is only the attitude you take in responding to life.

Unhealthy Attitude:
I have no choice. Life just happens to us.

ENERGY

Let each day
be your masterpiece.

Energy comes from deep within us. It comes out of a sense of curiosity: what is around the next corner? A sense of adventure: what will tomorrow hold? Interest in others: who are they? What do they think? Where are they going? As well, **energy comes from a desire to create our own destiny and make life more interesting and fulfilling.**

When I think of people with energy, I feel energised myself.

The best and most enduring example I have had in my life regarding energy has come from my mother. As a farmer's wife, my mother not only had to look after a family of seven (one child died of cancer at the age of nine, a heart-wrenching experience for any parent) she also undertook a lot of bookwork and organisation for the farm. In her 90s she still did the quarterly BAS (tax) statements and knew the price and cost of all the farm inputs and sales! As an incredibly busy mother and partner in the farming business, she did not overlook sport and leisure. She played copious amounts of golf and loved horseracing. While we were growing up, she drove us to every sporting event in our area and diligently sat and watched as we played tennis, basketball and participated in our school events. Not a bad effort when these schools were in some cases 300 kilometres apart!

Her biggest challenge in recent years was that she is physically unable to do all the housework in large chunks and could only work for short periods. She found that constraint frustrating but was philosophical about it. She had the satisfaction of knowing that she did all she could for as long as she could.

My mother had always had great curiosity about people and the planet. She had always been fully informed about world news, politics and even celebrity gossip! She had clear opinions which she has never shied away from and was never afraid to express them in front of her family — despite some clear differences of opinion!

In her late 80s, she underwent major heart surgery. Her purpose in doing so was that she would be there to look after my father whom she adored. I will never forget her telling me she was prepared to have this major and painful surgery. She just said, "I am going to do it and will be travelling by ambulance to the city tomorrow, so it can be done quickly."

Sadly my mother died during the writing

When I think of people with energy, I feel energised myself.

of this book but left so many amazing examples of her energy. The very day she was taken to hospital with a broken hip she had got up at 6.30 am at her own insistence, to help my brother make dozens of chicken sandwiches. As she started recovering from this debilitating surgery she desperately worked at rehab so that she could go back to the farm.

It was inspiring watching her working on getting her energy back and I know it will underpin my energy for the rest of my life. Sadly in the end, her weakened physical condition prevented her returning to her beloved farm. She left our family with a true understanding of living a life filled with energy and commitment.

On a less personal level, my favourite example of a man with energy is Sir Richard Branson. He seems to never stop adventuring and I love the way he has turned his business into a lifelong adventure.

Sometimes when I am in a city, I just stand and watch people go by. Some are so energised, some so disengaged—glum faces, bent backs, with the world on their shoulders. As we only get one go at this journey called life, I don't want to see mine slip into disengagement.

When I was working 24/7 growing a business and getting my business and financial life back on track, I was full of energy, due to the drive to get what I wanted and go where I wanted to go. Then I used to dream of retirement, of having enough money to never work again, envying those in that position. Now the word 'retirement' fills me with anxiety. I see many retired people who are very happy and relaxed, but more often I see retired people lacking a daily purpose.

It is this daily purpose that gives us energy.

Each day whenever possible, even in pouring rain, I start with a physical workout; a long walk, some cycling on a gym bike, some yoga moves (rather modified ones as they are memorised from a few yoga classes). I leave an hour in my day for this, and I always exercise in the morning. This morning energy comes from

life on a farm as a very young girl and then life in boarding school. Back in boarding school, I resented the relentless 6.30am bell rung by the generally unsmiling nun. In retrospect, I am quite grateful for being a morning person who is immediately able to deal with the challenges of the day.

However, I still have systems in place for those days when exercise is simply not an attractive idea. I place my walking gear beside my bed in such a way that I can easily and warmly dress, removing one of the myriad of excuses one can have for sleeping in! This habit however has a positive base for I really feel better after exercising in the morning.

I never travel without walking gear. It used to be jogging gear until my knees said enough! My dedication to exercise comes from a deep belief that our bodies and the way we treat them are so important.

For the same reason, my eating habits are quite disciplined as I see food as either energising or sluggifying (my new word!) We all know the foods that give us energy, help our system and make us feel great. These are not

Tips for Energy:

✓ Eat to give yourself energy— develop a healthy diet.

✓ Make daily exercise a priority.

✓ Mix with physically and mentally energetic people.

✓ Think forward to how you might feel if you could no longer be energetic. Will you feel you did all you could, for as long as you could?

the short—term comfort foods that all of us indulge in from time to time!

Energy, however, is not just related to our physical wellbeing for which we are all totally responsible. **Our energy also comes from our thoughts.**

We are what we think and what we eat. And the energy we feed ourselves comes from both healthy food and healthy thoughts.

Mixing with energetic, inspiring people is a great way to keep up the energy levels.

One of the reasons I love skiing in the US and, in fact anywhere, is because skiing is a high energy sport. As well as being high in the mountains, skiing attracts high energy people.

Aspen is my favourite resort for all these reasons. It is the town where people go to ski and party, where age is no barrier to either. In fact, there are many people in their 90s skiing in Aspen! The Aspen ski company has had to continually raise the Free Seniors skiing age, as people don't give up in Aspen.

The level of energy in this beautiful town has inspired me for years, even if sometimes the energy could be seen as ridiculous.

Recently, I was having my skis repaired in the early morning, I ran into a ski buddy who told me he was going to a lingerie party. He asked me to go with him. When I questioned him about a lingerie party in the morning he explained that, some 30 years ago, a group of gorgeous girls started the idea of turning up in ski suits and stripping down to *Victoria's Secrets* for a special breakfast in Aspen. They have kept this tradition alive and, although they are now in their 60s, they still have the energy, sense of fun and confidence to strip down to their lingerie!

I declined the invitation but could not help thinking with admiration that here is a group of women still proud of themselves and still having fun.

Each year I have left Aspen vowing to take the Aspen energy with me. When I feel a need to re-energise, I have only to think of the glorious blue skies, the Aspen trees and snow and how it feels to be in clear mountain air.

We all need to have a space in our hearts and minds that gives us energy.

Live with energy but don't take your eye off the ball.

Marcia,

I once listened to a sports psychologist talking about his work with top grade football players. Many of these young guys would tell him they were "pumped" for the big game. They were at their highest level of energy and ready to run out and take on the world!

He responded that he did not want them "pumped". Being "pumped" is likely to lead to a player not thinking at a crucial moment in the game as their concentration is filled with emotion rather than skill.

Perhaps that is where the 'all-in' brawl that can mar big games comes from. Players who are so "pumped" that they do not see the bigger picture, only their own emotions, until they are given a "yellow card" and have time to cool down!

In fact, what the sports psychologist really wanted them to do was to continue to perform their skills at the highest level. Being "pumped" can get in the way of doing the simple things right. The kick that is just too long, the pass that is "pushed" too quickly. No, good skills will win the day provided they are performed at the top level in the same way as they have been in training and as they have been in the past.

The same goes in life I would say. **If we do not take time to think deeply about our decisions and their meaning, we make mistakes** because we too were "pumped", over-emotional and convinced we are right.

I remember a young couple, married only a few months, who came seeking a signed form to say they could divorce.[7] One made the appointment but the other arrived early so that she would not have to be in the same room as the partner. She was so convinced it

was over. When the partner arrived he saw her behaviour as yet another example of her bad faith and continued broken promises.

Both were very angry, most certainly "pumped" and to have them in the same room might well have been a very volatile situation.

I am reluctant to sign a form that states a person has been to counselling, if that is the only thing we have focussed on in our session and it is the only session we ever have. However, I agreed with the couple to email a draft form to them for their separate approval. In that form I would state clearly, because that is part of the process, that both had attended but not together.

I sent the form. There was no reply. It was not sent back as approved by either of them!

Sometime later, they made a further appointment to work together on their relationship. By that time they were back together and planning a family. You see, making decisions based on emotional responses and not the whole human being will lead only to despair, not meaning.

Another example of being "pumped" and hence too hasty, is a client who told me how a few years back, he had been suicidal. He was convinced that he would end it all, had made plans and was about to take his life. Something in him, for none of us deep down want to die, made him call a crisis-call service. They put him on hold!

In fact, sick of waiting for someone to talk to, he hung up the phone and called back - three times in all, each time to be placed on hold! At that time he said to himself "bugger it, I'm going to bed".

Time is a great healer. What can seem an insurmountable problem today can in hindsight disappear from a mountain to a molehill.

Logotherapy, indeed any therapy, is not a "cure all." YOU must respond to where you are and what you can do NOW. But your response must be meaningful.

As I have pointed out before, it is a poor question to ask *What do I want from life?* There will always be a less than satisfactory answer. The real question to ask is *What does life ask of me—now, today?* That is where energy and attitude come into their own.

Attitude is only one of the three values that provide meaning in life, of course. The others are the capacity to create something in our lives and the capacity to experience life itself, in all its richness and in all its interactions with others.

The opposite to your concept of energy is that "existential vacuum", that listless, lack of meaning in life that can lead to boredom, addictions and depression.

You mention your desire to create your own destiny. We all need to have that and I defined 'destiny' as a logotherapy concept in the previous chapter.

What an understanding of "destiny" does is to provide a daily purpose in life for us, what we call the 'meaning of the moment'. It can be as simple as looking after the children or going to work in order to make sure the family is supported. It is often easy to discern. The children must be fed, the lawn mown, I need to go to work on time. All reasonably easy "moments" of meaning.

For most of us the 'meaning of the moment' does take energy, perhaps considerable amounts of it. We can allow this daily grind of work to sap our energy and emotions or we can decide that, no matter what, it simply will not grind us down. That is attitude.

You were challenged by this when you were working so hard to grow a business and dreaming of retirement. In other words, dreaming that one day you would not have to respond quite so vigorously to life's challenges. The danger is that, in dreaming of a future like this, you end up with a life in which you lose sight of your meaning day by day, moment by moment.

I note that you have not retired! You realised that retiring in life is not possible. Retiring in this sense is not ceasing to work. It is ceasing to want to respond. In fact, that is a choice in itself but its result is listlessness, boredom and lack of meaning.

You continue to be inventive. You continue to exercise. Both of these recognise that the body and the mind are important. However, the most important part of the human person is the core self, our very 'essence' or, at the risk of sounding religious, our 'spirit', our "essence", that very human capacity to rise above what confronts us.

You see, we must strive always to have this energy and respond to life's challenge, even to the very end. **We have to realise that life always has a meaning, even in its most difficult times.**

Does a terminally ill patient have a meaning? Yes, even that person. Life is asking a significant question, to which the only answer may be the attitude that is taken to life's limitations at that time.

Deepak Chopra has a concept that every living cell is eavesdropping on the mind. Let's go beyond this. The human person is a whole being. So it is certainly true that our very attitude affects both the mind and the body. If we are left with nothing else, it is our attitude and our desire to find meaning in our lives and to accept where we are. This acceptance will itself provide the energy that we need.

What happens when life seems to have no meaning? People simply give up. On the other hand, they may decide to seek some sort of rock to hang on to — a certainty which is often found in fundamentalist beliefs. There are also those, young people in particular, who may become aggressive and resort to violence.

Logotherapy challenges us to find the meaning in life wherever we are. It challenges us to realise that it is life itself that asks questions of us, constantly asking *What will you do with this situation right now?*

It is the answer to that question that requires, and indeed produces, energy.

Healthy Attitude:
What does life challenge me to be or do now, today?

Unhealthy Attitude:
What do I want from life?

Healthy Attitude:
Every life is unique and has its own meaning.

Unhealthy Attitude:
I am not important.

Healthy Attitude:
I continue to wonder about the meaning of my life. Is there any ultimate meaning?

Unhealthy Attitude:
Life has no meaning.

RESILIENCE

It's not what happens to you that matters,
it's what you do about
what happens that matters.

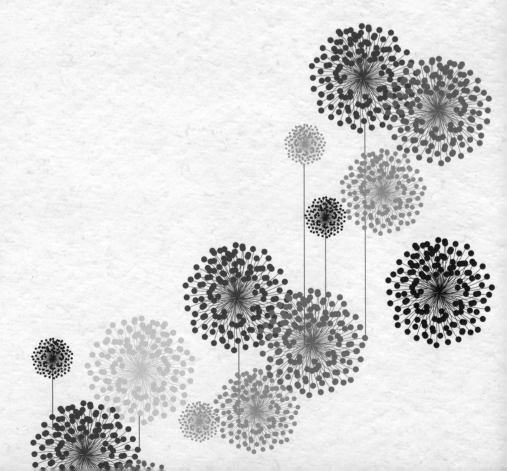

Resilience is the power or ability to return to original form after being bent or compressed or, as I have heard it defined, the 'bounce back' factor. This seems to me to be one of the most powerful abilities we can have in life.

This is the quality that enables us to take the challenges and knocks in life and literally bounce back from them. One thing we can be very sure of in life is that each of us will have challenges we need to bounce back from.

Recently I saw a segment on television that showed the recovery of a footballer who had his neck broken during a game and became a paraplegic. He made a commitment to himself and his family that he would walk again. After 25 years of incredible effort he can now walk again and is thinking about marathons. Some bounce-back factor!

How does one acquire this?

We live in a society that tends to crush rather than encourage personal resilience, so we really need to work at getting and keeping the bounce back factor.

Throughout history, government handouts and the nanny state have been proven to not work, yet the same is happening in Australia right now. Australia is a country built on the resilience of the pioneers, the explorers, the settlers. These men and women who shaped this country had to deal with all sort of crises on their own: fires, floods, disease. Due to the harshness of their environment and the lack of facilities, they had no choice but to develop many personal qualities, not the least of which was the ability to face, deal with and overcome challenges of all sorts.

In our world today, there are many amazing examples of resilience. Every time I hear stories from Afghanistan, Syria and other trouble spots on the planet, I think of the people affected and the resilience they will need to recuperate from lost limbs, lost families, lost houses etc. Each time I visit Israel and see that how that small piece of desert has been transformed into a green power-house of ideas and talent, impacting on the whole world – I feel inspired. Paralympians are another great example of an incredible group of people who have fought back and taken control of disabilities and achieved great heights of physical and mental prowess. And the list goes on.

On the other hand, in the western world we have an estimated one in six taking some form of anti-depressant. I wonder if this helps people develop a bounce back factor or simply dulls this ability by dulling the problem?

At one point in my life, I had to face a series of critical issues. In a short space of time, I had to face the fact that I was unable to have children, my marriage was on the rocks and I had to face the challenge of losing my house and all my assets. My initial reaction to all this was self-pity: "Poor me! Why me? I did not deserve this" and the ensuing self-talk that takes us down a very negative track.

At that time, I was extremely fortunate to meet a man who persuaded me that I had abilities that were unused; that I would be great at, of all things, sales. So with a great deal of initial resistance and doubt, I started a new journey in my life which took me on track to revived self-esteem and personal strength.

Looking back, I realise that I had resilience from an early age. Boarding school life at the age of eleven is an amazing way to learn to bounce back on one's own as there was no back up family to blow noses or hold one's hand. Boarding school was a tough environment and I think there are better ways to learn resilience!

Actually my new career in sales, after life in the corporate world, was a great lesson in dealing with knocks, negatives and in some cases derision: *Why would someone like you be selling cosmetics?*

My first attempts at selling or 'persuading' someone to hold a sales presentation at their house were, to say the least, unsuccessful. I called thirty women I knew before someone finally said, "Yes, I am happy to have my friends over to see these products!" During the process, I was overwhelmed with self-doubt. As each call turned into a negative response, I felt myself questioning the wisdom of my new career time and time again.

Voices told me: "Go back to the safety of the corporate world; you don't know anything about selling; do something where you will get a decent salary which you need right now!" On and on the voices went. They seemed to make sense, but I kept on thinking about the new world I was venturing into, and the challenge of selling something unknown in Australia. Somehow it was that challenge that captured my attention.

My challenge was, of course, nothing compared to the challenge of millions of others around the world: those who wake up each day searching for food; those being persecuted for their beliefs; refugees struggling to start a new life; people with health issues trying to survive; and so the list of true battlers goes on. When we are in the middle of life's challenges, the problems of others are no consolation to us, because we lose perspective and are unable to see the positives and the possibilities.

All of us need the bounce-back factor because, apart from the certainty of death, all of us will and do face challenges that require enormous resilience. We will all at some stage give in to feelings of depression, hopelessness, failure and even fear of success. It is our ability to bounce back that determines how we overcome and survive.

Everyone has those days where it all seems too much. We need to recognise that and believe that we will get through.

Tips for Resilience:

✔ Exercise daily to build up physical and mental strength.

✔ Don't expect life to be easy every day — it simply is not for anyone!

✔ Take on challenges that stretch you, so that you work on your self-esteem and your strengths.

✔ Read about, listen to and learn from people who have developed the bounce back factor. Make those people your heroes.

✔ Chunk problems down into bite size pieces and tackle them one-by-one.

Logotherapy and resilience

Marcia,

Talking about resilience is an excellent way to conclude our conversations about life and logotherapy. **Resilience, the capacity to rise again and respond to life, is at the heart of it all.**

I have pointed out elsewhere that most therapeutic approaches focus on trying to take the client's mind off disturbed or disturbing modes of experience and to provide stability. That has its place, don't get me wrong. However, it does not provide a 'cure'. What does so, often without the therapist actually working directly on this, is a change of attitude to life itself.

A recent client of mine came because he had heard about logotherapy and that he needed to experience it. This is a little unusual, as in most of my work while I do use a logotherapeutic approach because it fits over the top or alongside of virtually all other approaches to therapy, I only rarely instruct the client in its basic philosophy of life or view of the human being.

It can also be problematic when a client comes for "logotherapy" because they want to find a meaning for life. Step one is sometimes to help the client understand that I cannot give them meaning in life – they must search for it, and I will try to walk beside them as they do so.

This client had lost everything as a result of the Global Financial Crisis. His business, his house, and in some ways his filial relations as his siblings and parents had all invested in the business. Literally he had nothing. He had not chosen to go bankrupt, as some of his advisors advocated, but to pay out his creditors because his personal integrity demanded this.

A friend loaned a car, another allowed him to live with his wife and children in a small townhouse until he found a job and began to earn some income. He thought about suicide but he decided his wife and kids were too important to him. His doctor diagnosed depression and prescribed the appropriate medication. My client took it once only and then decided that this was not for him.

I agreed, his real problem was not depression but the challenge presented by life itself. I told him in fact that he had probably already solved his problem as he was determined to rebuild his life, establish another business and make sure this time he did not over-reach and that over time he could repay the family.

But he had learned a significant lesson. He told me a few times during our sessions together that his friends in the business world still spoke as though they measured "success" but what they owned, how much they earned and their perceived status in society. As he said, "they just don't get it, do they?"

Logotherapy is about helping clients to realise their human capacity to bring out the best in themselves. It challenges them to use their free will and responsibility to take a stand, to take meaningful decisions. It challenges them to realise that there will always be a healthy tension in a life well lived—a decision to take one direction will prevent me from taking another.

So resilience, or the capacity for lasting change, requires a meaning-filled approach to life. In fact, if the therapist centres their work only on cognitions and behaviours, then the deeper dimension of the real human being, their essence, their core capacity to respond to life and what it asks of them will be left to the client.

I am reminded of an interesting study that brings this out very clearly. It followed up 99 alcohol dependent men in London, 10-22 years after treatment, to identify what they felt had caused improvement in their situation.[8]

They said:

* Taking an interest in other people

* Thinking what I could do for my family if sober

* Feeling able to give love

* Spouse's unhappiness over my drinking

* Working very hard at my job

* Reactions of my children to my drinking

* Getting a new job

In other words, they found meaning. If only they could have been helped by a logotherapist this may have been a quicker process, although there are no guarantees. A logotherapist cannot find your meaning; only help you to do so.

Logotherapy is very much about the capacity we all have to take a stand in the face of adversity. This may not mean going back to where you were or being as materially well off as you once were. That may happen, but the core of logotherapy is the attitude you take to life and adversity.

Life is full of decisions but most of them are small, insignificant and day to day. Most of them are a little like floating on a placid ocean. However, there are times when the tide goes out and the reef that lies beneath the surface is exposed a little. When that happens we can no longer just float placidly. We have to move and the decisions can be painful.

To accept all of this creates all types of opportunities. Yes, as I said the exposed reef was potentially painful and that is a challenge. But every challenge creates an opportunity – good business planning recognises this. The opportunity is that even in the face of adversity you now have the capacity to shape the future, starting from today. This is your destiny.

Destiny is not what has already been determined, or something pre-planned for us from the beginning of time. No, destiny is the choice and the path we all strive to take, but starting from where we now.

One comforting feature of logotherapy is the foundational belief that life has meaning under any and all circumstances. However, this truth is also confronting. It provides us with a stark choice: what we do now is what can provide meaning in life. Logotherapy cannot provide a meaning for you, only you can do that. You can't be told

what your destiny is, but you can have a significant say in what it might be.

I understand your comments on the 'nanny state'. The biggest challenge for the therapist is to help people realise they cannot 'have it all'. It seems sometimes that our politicians and leaders do not want to tell us that truth.

We must experience a range of challenges and emotions that are a part of being human. If we were never sad how would we realise what happiness is? If we were never a bit "down" how would we understand the elation of reaching a goal?

We need contrasting experiences if we are to be fully the person we are destined to be. We have all faced life's challenges in the past, but may not always remember that we have done so and that we have been resilient. The task of the therapist is to uncover these 'victory moments', so that the person can start to believe in themselves.

Stephen Southwick, in his book *Resilience*,[9] examines the medical and psychological realities of resilience under the headings:

❉ Optimism

❉ Facing fear

❉ Moral compass

❉ Religion and spirituality

❉ Social support

❉ Role models

❉ Physical fitness

❉ Brain fitness

❉ Cognitive and emotional flexibility

All of these are important attributes for anyone seeking to simply respond to life's challenges. The more of them we have, the more well-placed we will be to be resilient. They do run parallel to most of the topics we have addressed in our conversations.

It is significant that Southwick's final chapter is titled *Meaning and Purpose*. That is the core of logotherapy; helping the client search for that in life.

Remember, not having challenges in life, not setting goals for ourselves and finding that we do not have tasks to complete, leads to frustration and boredom. This is what Frankl termed the 'existential vacuum'. It is all-pervading in our society. Those who fall prey to it will simply sink into despair when the reef is exposed at the ebb-tides of life.

Healthy Attitude:
Life is about change. There will always be a new challenge to be faced.

Unhealthy Attitude:
I don't want to change; it's too hard.

Healthy Attitude:
Being the best I can be needs daily effort.

Unhealthy Attitude:
I'm okay as I am.

Healthy Attitude:
What I do today is the only thing I can control.

Unhealthy Attitude:
My life has been affected by past experiences.

ATTITUDE OF GRATITUDE

Have an attitude of gratitude;
never forget those who
helped you along the way.

After eleven years of university life and degrees, I was totally amazed to hear from an uneducated but streetwise person that, as important as university degrees are, attitude is even more important! In those eleven years I had never had any lecturer, either in philosophy classes or my later commerce studies, mention the importance of attitude in having a fulfilled life and successful business.

As I left the confines and protectiveness of corporate life and ventured into the world of sales, I had to continually focus on this word 'attitude'. I found it annoying sometimes when I was told the solution to achievement in sales was solely related to having a positive attitude.

Going through divorce, facing up to financial disaster, not being able to have children all seemed to me at the time good reason not to have a positive attitude.

I read books about attitude and often found them cheesy and unrealistic. I remember taking a friend along to hear one of the famous American motivational speakers and, while I was impressed, my friend just could not go along with what she found to be a very over the top approach to being positive.

Over the years, as I dug my way out of the financial and emotional issues resulting from divorce, I found that, to succeed, **I definitely needed to have a positive attitude. And the basis of that would need to be an attitude of gratitude.**

I had to focus on the positives and examine, learn from, and move on from the negatives. I had to be grateful for opportunities, rather than focus on the negatives—and there were plenty of those. Direct-selling is a great way to discover one's strength and weaknesses as, in making the sale, there is complete dependence on the reactions of potential customers — people!

Just as I felt that I had moved up a step in the business, a negative customer reaction would pull me back. I realised I had to build a solid base for my positive thinking that could not be buffeted by the reactions of those around me. If I was to regain my self-esteem and succeed in my business life and life generally, I needed to have something which would sustain my positive thinking and enable me to deal with the negatives.

My mentor during this time was someone who'd had much less of a start in life than I had. He had not been to a private school, he had not lived on a wonderful farm as a child, he had not ridden ponies to school, he had not been to university, he had not travelled the world as a young adventurer, and yet he seemed to keep moving on with this life, despite many challenges.

I realised that he had the attitude of gratitude that I needed to develop and focus on. This attitude did not come naturally to me. While I had certainly not been indulged as a

child, nor had I been deprived, so I had not had to think about being grateful for what I had. But later in life when things went awry, I seriously had to work on developing an attitude of gratitude, by focusing on what I had rather than what I had lost or what others had.

This thinking really started working for me and I have maintained it ever since. I now see very clearly the dissatisfaction which occurs in our affluent society when people focus on what others have, rather than the opportunities they themselves have.

It's called 'keeping up with the Joneses'. It's a very unhealthy and dissatisfying way to live life. It's also expensive, often wasteful and generally pointless.

I remember being in New York once at sale time, standing in the very upmarket store Bergdorf Goodman, as I watched women fighting over dresses. None of these women looked as though they needed another dress but there they were attacking each other! There is a wonderful saying that I keep in the back of my mind –*You can never have enough of what you don't need*.

I recently watched a movie starring Demi Moore called *The Joneses*. It was a surprisingly deep movie with a clear message. Keeping up with the Joneses is destructive, costly and can end badly!

Sometimes it takes a big change in one's life to get this message: that we own our own journey and, at the end of the road looking back on our lives, we have to live with the regrets, the successes and the things that have given us deep satisfaction.

Every day now, I think about how fortunate I am — starting with my good health, with the fact that I live in and was born in Australia, that I can now pay my bills and live the life I want within reason. I am grateful that I have worked hard to achieve financial

independence; that I don't have a need to have everything that many richer people around me have; that I feel a deep sense of peace and happiness when I walk along a beach and witness a stunning sunset. **I am grateful and inspired by the great people on the planet — who may be either high achievers or simply battlers who get on with life and give more than they take.**

My attitude of gratitude makes me feel lucky and underpins a deep positivity.

Tips for Attitude of Gratitude:

✓ Focus on what you have, rather than what you don't have.

✓ Find things to be grateful for each day.

✓ Become aware of the environment around you—start noticing the little things.

✓ Think about where you sit in the pecking order of humanity and be grateful.

Be Grateful for Meaning

Marcia,

I have been grateful to you throughout the book for your personal insights and for the opportunity to respond to them as a therapist. An attitude of gratitude is the key to coping successfully with life. It is not the only answer, as this book points out. However, it is the key that opens doors. Bracing yourself with an attitude to go through those doors opens the way for this book to affect your life.

Remember always:

❋ Disappointments are inevitable.

❋ Misery is always optional.

I enjoyed reading how your mentor taught you to focus on the positives in life. If we allow it to do so, gratitude makes sense of our past, brings peace for today and can create a vision for tomorrow.

It is never too late to reflect back to see how positively life has treated us. We have been spared many things, and that is the real definition of good fortune, not what "lady luck" has brought us, but what we have not been challenged to endure.

In 1981, Albert Facey published *A Fortunate Life*, his autobiography of experiences during the Gallipoli campaign and of growing up in an environment that gave him lots of hard knocks. It is what many would see as an extraordinary life of hardship, loss, friendship and love. Yet he called it *A Fortunate Life*. When asked why he did so, he replied that he really believed that his life was fortunate.

On the other hand, Facey endured many hardships. The story begins with him being born in Victoria in 1894 and follows on with the death of his father only two years later. It was not long before he was left by his mother in the care of his grandmother. His early life included working on farms at eight years of age with little education and being unable to read or write. He taught himself to do so.

I could go on. However, **the important lesson is that we can all look back and summarise life by listing those things for which we can be grateful.**

I had one client who came in distress from just being weighed down by coping with life. A husband who was "non-threatening" but also a non-contributor; an aging mother who drifted in and out of dementia but when lucid was just a carping critic for everything she did; a mortgage incurred because she had generously helped her son out of difficulties and was repaid only with more requests for help.

Meanwhile she had a job that demanded 50 or more hours each week, with less than 40 actually paid, and the job itself looked like being declared redundant. She assessed he current situation as hopeless, indeed disastrous.

She did tell me proudly that she had eight children and twenty grandchildren, but almost in the same breath added that she wished she had never come to Australia from England with her parents. "I wish I had never set foot in this country!", she said strongly. My reply was "so you wish you had never had twenty grandchildren?" "Well, if you put it like that... no" she replied. **You see, there will always be things we are grateful for, even despite the harshness of real life.**

What are you grateful for?

Can you list ten things in life for which you are grateful? If you have really understood the message of this book then you will have no trouble with this list, and not all of them will be positive. That you are alive and reading this book is perhaps the first!

1. _____

2. _____

3. _____

4. _____

5. _____

6. _____

7. _____

8. _____

9. _____

10. _____

How many times have you agonised about a coming event or commitment and it actually turned out to be positive? How many times have wonderful things entered your life at what seems to be just the right time, with no particular effort on your part? This is certainly true for me. This book for instance.

Marcia, your introduction suggests that when the student is ready, the teacher will appear. I felt you were very kind to describe me in that way. From my own perspective, just at the time that I was ready to spread the message of hope that is the message of logotherapy, and to invite all Australians to reconnect with meaning, along you came with all your energy and enthusiasm.

The rest is history. We have a book that meshes together the experience of a wonderful achiever in business and the concepts of logotherapy that run parallel to an attitude of success. Logotherapy defines success a little differently, as you would have read in the various chapters.

So yes, Marcia, attitude is certainly a key to achievement and living but it has to be an **attitude of gratitude.** Compare some more healthy and unhealthy attitudes.

Having an attitude of gratitude is largely an issue of training yourself to have it. It is the capacity to simply view life by looking through a positive lens.

"There are only two ways to live your life. One is as though nothing is a miracle. The other is as though everything is a miracle."

—Albert Einstein

Healthy attitude:
I have freedom.

Unhealthy attitude:
I am a victim of 'fate.'

Healthy attitude:
I need to become responsible.

Unhealthy attitude:
The chief aim of life is to heighten my pleasure and reduce my discomfort.

Healthy attitude:
I will live according to my values.

Unhealthy attitude:
I will live according to whatever feels good at the moment.

THE STORY BEHIND THIS BOOK

Life is both chosen
and accidental.

The famous Motorway Motel!

I feel that I should describe how I met my co-author, as the story has shades of so much that we have talked about in this book.

As I mentioned previously, after reading *Man's Search for Meaning* **I felt a real need to explore logotherapy** and find out where it was being taught and used to help people get through challenges in their lives.

So, of course, I googled Logotherapy Australia (I thought it best to start in my own country) and found the name of an academic at the University of Adelaide. I emailed this person and explained my mission: I wanted to learn more about logotherapy and I wanted to meet psychologists and/or psychiatrists who were using this positive, powerful method with their patients and clients.

The Adelaide contact mentioned that a psychologist, Dr Paul McQuillan in Brisbane, was developing a training course in logotherapy and seeking accreditation for it.

This sounded promising so I emailed Dr Paul McQuillan and explained my interest in contacting him. We emailed each other a number of (in fact many) times, and he gave me some dates for a course in logotherapy he was teaching some months down the track. This was to be a two-day course aimed at chaplains and counsellors.

The course was being held in the far west of Brisbane, an area that I knew nothing about. So I asked Paul if he could recommend accommodation there. He emailed back that there was very limited accommodation in this area but there was a motel not too far away from the location of the training course. As the course was some time away, I headed for one of those internet accommodation sites and booked three nights at the Motorway Motel.

Life was extremely busy at this time, so I did not consider the matter further and sometime later booked the cheapest flight from Melbourne to Brisbane. As the time got closer, I revisited the accommodation site and the motel looked like a typical three star Australian model — not very inviting but okay.

I arrived at Brisbane airport at midnight on a Friday and did have some misgivings when the taxi driver estimated that a ride to the motel where I had booked for three nights would be around $80 plus — quite a long taxi ride, even by expensive Australian standards!

As we got further and further from the Brisbane city skyline with which I was very familiar, and headed off on a very industrialised highway, my heart starting sinking. My memories of travel adventures from the past came back — backpacking around Asia, hitchhiking through Europe. But this time I was in Australia, what was I doing here anyway? **Who was this Dr Paul McQuillan? He read well, but who was he really?**

My feelings of concern were elevated as we left the barren highway and circled back towards a motel with missing letters on the sign, surrounded by large empty transport trucks. This was truly the sort of place that one might see in an American movie, where the director is trying to create a feeling of ominous fear in the audience!

I felt quite sick inside, but could see that a man was sitting inside the tiny reception area and he looked as though he might have been waiting for someone to arrive. I had to quickly choose: stay in the taxi, go back to a Sheraton

or some such in the city, or stay for the night?

I decided on the latter, paid the taxi driver, got out into the darkness and headed to reception, a glorified description for a tiny room with a few red plastic, frayed chairs.

Yes, the man had been waiting for me, as I was the last to check in for the night. He took my credit card details for the extras I might be spending and pointed out my room. He said the entrance was around the corner, so I asked him to stay in reception until he saw my light, as it was totally dark and lonely.

I walked with trepidation around the corner and noticed that the vehicle parked outside the door beside mine was one of those covered utilities with blackened windows — not the sort of vehicle that makes one feel confident about one's neighbours. I opened the door as quickly as possible and turned on all lights, checked for locks on the windows and door and put the chain across. The room was as grim as the exterior indicated; this was not a place women would willingly stay on their own.

I got into bed quickly, vowing that I would be out of there at dawn!

Fortunately, I have learnt the art of sleeping well as a traveller and did so. My early inspection of the room next morning held no surprises. The room was clean but extremely shabby, with cracked tiles, a very old towel and a bedside lamp that had lost its globe. My decision was easy—not to return after Paul came to collect me, as he had promised to do.

I took photos of the many defects and the transports parked outside. I rang the internet booking company and explained my dilemma: I could not stay here for three nights; this was

not a place for a woman on her own. The response was that I would need to take the matter up with the manager, to get a refund for the next two nights.

With photos in hand, I approached the same man in reception that I had met the night before. I explained that I simply could not spend the weekend here. He was at first reluctant and suggested I change rooms. I explained that it was the place and lonely location more than the room that worried me. I should also mention that I did say that, should we not come to an agreement, I would go back to the internet booking site with a very, very bad review, with photos of the surrounding trucks and cracked tiles to prove my point. Finally he agreed, we shook hands and the Motorway Motel avoided trending badly on Twitter!

This was, after all, a place for transport drivers used to lonely, out of the way overnight stops. I stood waiting for Paul outside the motel, bag packed and ready to leave.

On first meeting Paul, I had huge trust in him and we laughed all the way to the course venue about his accommodation recommendation, which he again assured me was based simply on proximity to where we needed to go.

The next two days of intensive logotherapy introduction were stimulating and enlightening.

There is nothing more empowering for the human spirit than the belief that we all have deep within us the power we need to make our lives meaningful and fulfilling.

So often in my travels, trips that start badly have ended well. This was to be no exception.

Footnotes

[1] Neurosis — a former name for a category of mental disorders in which the symptoms are distressing to the person, reality testing is intact, behaviour does not violate gross social norms, and there is no apparent organic cause. In current terminology they are termed 'disorders'.

[2] "Man's Search for Meaning", Beacon Edition 2006, p. 109

[3] See Logo talk radio No 54. This can be searched readily on the web and provides a good overview of many logotherapy concepts

[4] Failure of muscular coordination; irregularity of muscular action

[5] See *The Will to Meaning* – Self transcendence as a human phenomenon.

[6] Man's Search for Meaning", Beacon Edition (2006), p. 15

[7] In Australia divorce is a "no fault" process and all the couple need to do is to show they have been separated for 12 months or more. However, if they have been married less than 12 months in the first place this does not apply in the same way. They need to have a form signed by a counsellor to state that they have both been to counselling about the relationship or that at the very least one has tried but the other refused to take part.

[8] Edwards, G, Brown, D, Duckitt, A, Oppenheimer, E, Sheehan, M, & Taylor, C (1987) 'Outcome of Alcoholism: the structure of patient attributions as to what causes change.' British Journal of Addiction, 82, pp533-545

[9] Southwick, S.M. & Charney, D.S. (2012). *Resilience: The science of mastering life's greatest challenges.*

Index

Balance – 81, 82, 83, 84, 85, 86, 87, 88, 89

Conscience – 31, 32, 42, 52, 60, 61, 62, 63, 69, 109

Decisions – 17, 36, 42, 43, 45, 46, 47, 48, 49, 50, 51, 52, 53, 60, 61, 62, 63, 70, 85, 96, 99, 108, 109, 126, 127, 134, 135, 143, 144

Energy – 79, 130, 131, 132, 133, 134, 135, 136, 137

Exercise – 84, 131, 132, 133, 136, 141

Fate – 78, 96, 97, 99, 108, 127, 153

Gratitude – 148, 149, 150, 152

Integrity – 9, 55, 56, 57, 59, 60, 61, 63, 67, 69, 142

Learning – 36, 73, 74, 75, 76, 77, 78, 79, 94, 103, 107

Logotherapy – 13, 14, 15, 16, 17, 22, 30, 31, 40, 41, 43, 50, 51, 52, 60, 68, 76, 78, 79, 86, 88, 117, 119, 124, 125, 135, 136, 142, 143, 144, 145, 152, 156, 157

Optimism – 20, 21, 22, 23, 40, 145

Perspective – 67, 111, 112, 113, 114, 115, 116, 117, 118, 119, 141

Purpose – 26, 27, 28, 29, 30, 31, 32, 33, 95, 109, 130, 131, 136

Resilience – 9, 139, 140, 141, 142, 143, 144, 145

Responsibility – 9, 28, 31, 35, 36, 37, 38, 39, 40, 41, 42, 43, 48, 49, 63, 67, 70, 85, 117, 143

Risk – 74, 85, 91, 92, 93, 94, 95, 96, 97, 98, 99, 103, 108

Self-belief – 95, 101, 102, 103, 104, 105, 107, 108, 109

Uniqueness – 5, 13, 15, 17, 31, 33, 42, 53, 60, 61, 62, 63, 65, 66, 67, 68, 69, 70, 71, 95, 106, 118, 137

Viktor Frankl – 8, 14, 21, 29, 30, 50

Vision – 121, 122, 123, 124, 125, 126, 127, 140, 150

Endorsements from around the world

Sheds a vivid new light on the work of Viktor Frankl – on the one hand, and gives a life size example for every woman – on the other. I find this book very important from many aspects; not to mention the politics of identity perspective. Marcia Griffin is an inspiration to women everywhere. She is one of those people who encourage others to believe in themselves and achieve. This book is a gem!

—Nira Tessler (Ph.D.) is a lecturer on the history of art and design at various Israeli academic institutions in Israel.

Fascinating! What a relief to read an excerpt that goes beyond the concrete and the "how to" strategies; to address the more meaningful and fulfilling internal driving force that moves you from the robotic functioning to healthy and purposeful choices. I also found the approach practical and useful as it grounds the theory into the practical business and personal day to day journey.

—Greg Farrugia, Psychologist, Brisbane.

Leaders from two different worlds. Paul and Marcia click in an enlightening and entertaining dialogue that communicates real life wisdom. While the topics are timeless, the authors' discussion is at once contemporary and approachable. Readers will be taken on a unique journey with a payoff that can last a lifetime.

—Marshall H. Lewis, Ph.D., Associate Editor, The International Forum for Logotherapy, USA.

An easy to read book which focuses on practical, self-help for attaining a more fulfilling and purposeful life through a conversational approach would have broad appeal. Done through a framework of Logotherapy based on Viktor Frankl's principles, readers can gain a deeper understanding of self on life's journey through deeper insights into one's motivations, purposes and life's paradoxes.

—Dr. Eugene Kaminski, Deputy Dean of Education (ret.), Australian Catholic University.

The insights of Logotherapy get to the heart of human motivation and human fulfilment. This book makes those insights accessible to people living busy lives in the busy world of business.

—The Revd Canon Professor Leslie J Francis
Professor of Religions and Education Warwick Religions and Education Research Unit, United Kingdom

The work of Viktor Frankl is brought to life in this stimulating book by Paul and Marcia. Meaning, including its search, is core to our being and transcends much of what is offered in leadership and management development programs which are often faddish in nature. This book will appeal to a broad audience, but executive coaches, leaders, and counsellors will gain great value from absorbing its contents.

—Peter Macqueen, Psychologist (Organisational, Fellow,
Institute of Management Consultants (Australia), Fellow of the Australian Psychological Society

The authors have found an unusual yet effective means to introduce Victor Frankl's most central ideas to readers. By engaging in dialogue, they bring to life what Frankl wanted people to know, such as the concept of purpose as the engine that fires action and leads to fulfilling lives. This book promises an engaging and informative read.

—Dr. Angela Ebert
Head of Postgraduate Counselling Programs, Murdoch University

This is a timely book that draws on the lived experience of the authors. Readers are encouraged to reflect more deeply on what is important for them and their lives, and so live life more fully, healthily and happily.

Barry Buckley, Educationist, Australia, Principal Emeritus St Joseph's College Gregory Terrace, Brisbane.